Weird Things in History and Why the Heck They Happened

Funny Stories of Weird History of the World and Fun Facts Everyone Should Know Just Because

PABLO VANNUCCI

ISBN: 9798395464200

DEDICATION

For all those people who thought they were
made of glass, I raise my glass to you.
Thank you for inspiring this book.

CONTENTS

INTRODUCTION

Welcome to *Weird Things in History and Why the Heck They Happened* where we explore some bizarre and just plain peculiar historical events you may or may not have heard of. We invite you to join us on a journey that will be funny, insightful, and downright weird.

For example, four score and seven years ago was an electrifying decade of weirdness called the 1930s. A poltergeist in the form of a talking mongoose took over a farmhouse and attracted ghost hunters from all over. The Dymaxion car debuted as a concept car with three wheels and room for 11 passengers. A Dutch warship pretended to be a tropical island to avoid an attack. And the word "dord" mistakenly entered the dictionary as an abbreviation for density.

The 1930s were undoubtedly a decade of strange events, but this book isn't just about this decade. It's about exploring the oddities of history from all across time and discovering events that slipped through the spines of our history books.

But why do we find these weird historical events so fascinating? Perhaps it's because they remind us that history is not just dry facts and figures but also about the people and events that shape our modern world. Delving into the forgotten cracks of history to find the interesting and the unusual is what makes history fun. The events we explore here, from pineapple jewelry and vampire redheads to creepy doll inventions and cats turned telephone, will leave you scratching your head and wondering why on earth these things ever happened in the first place.

Each weird event, or each chapter, comes in three parts. Part 1, called "The Fact," explains the weird historical event. Part 2 is called "The Story," where we'll take a deep dive into the specific circumstances surrounding the event, the historical setting, the people involved, and why it has the honor of popping up in a book dedicated to all things weird history. Part 3 is called "The Breakdown," where we'll fast forward to the present and look at the impact the historical event may have on our world today and any lessons we can learn from it.

Many of these weird events are downright hilarious, so we couldn't pass up the opportunity to spoof some of them. Six of the 25 weird events in this book have a fourth part, which we call "The Sketch." These are short stories parodying the event that take place in a fictitious setting with fictitious characters. They're a comedic peek into how the weird event could have played out if we were there ourselves. We hope you enjoy them!

So, are you ready for your weird history lesson? We promise to take you on an informative, entertaining, and perhaps a little unsettling journey. Because sometimes, the weirder things in history are the ones that teach us the most about ourselves and our world.

CHAPTER 1:
GREAT MOON HOAX

Part 1: The Fact

In 1835, a small New York City newspaper broke the most shocking news: there was life on the moon! The six-part series of articles documenting the supposed discovery of life and civilization on the moon that was published in *The Sun* was what came to be known as the "Great Moon Hoax."

Part 2: The Story

Everyone thought the articles were real. People must have believed everything they read in 1835. According to these articles, Sir John Herschel, a great astronomer of the time, used a huge telescope to find evidence of life on the moon. Several of these articles claimed Herschel observed exotic creatures on the moon, including unicorns, beavers, and even creatures resembling humans. The essay continued to describe a lunar society with giant trees, lush vegetation, and oceans filled with life.

Of course, the articles captured the attention of the entire world. You had to be pretty dull not to perk up at the news that there were beavers on the moon. Readers eagerly waited for each new installment of the amazing story. It was a sensation that helped create a newfound interest in astronomy and space travel.

In reality, the Great Moon Hoax was the result of a group of newspaper writers' strong imaginations who wanted to increase circulation for their little newspaper and make a quick buck. It was ironic the articles in *The Sun* were about life on the moon and not on the sun. That would have been a much better marketing strategy. Sir John Herschel wasn't involved with the hoax in any way, either. He made no discoveries about our moon during his career, but he did play a role in naming four moons of Uranus and seven moons of Saturn.

Part 3: The Breakdown

The excitement in 1835 pretty much stopped at square dances and berry-picking socials, so why were people so quick to believe that unicorns and especially beavers lived on the moon? A portion of it was timing. The 1830s saw significant scientific and technical developments, and people were eager to learn more about the cosmos. Furthermore, the idea of extraterrestrial life hadn't yet been completely ruled out as science fiction. The Great Moon Hoax played on people's excitement with the idea there might be life on other planets. It serves as a reminder of how people have been intrigued by the secrets of the universe for a very long time.

Fun fact: A story about winged people living on the moon was published in the *New York Sun* a year before, but it didn't capture the public's attention in the same way as the Great Moon Hoax. Beavers on the moon must have been a much more realistic concept than winged people.

There are a lot of similar Great Moon Hoax stories in our world today. We're constantly exposed to spectacular headlines and fake news articles on the internet and social media. The Great Moon Hoax serves as a warning to never lose our capacity for skepticism and to proceed with caution when reading startling news. If we read a news story today about unicorns and beavers on the moon, we'd know right away it was just a story. You have to admit though, it would be fun to imagine beavers floating around up there, if only for a moment.

CHAPTER 2:
1904'S MESSY MARATHON

Part 1: The Fact

Many people see the Olympics as the height of human athleticism and sportsmanship. The world's top athletes come together to compete against one another every four years. However, the 1904 Olympics in St. Louis, Michigan were a bit unusual, particularly the marathon competition. The stories that came out of that race were both intriguing and odd. In short, the marathon was a complete mess.

Part 2: The Story

Picture the scene. It was August. The temperature sweltered above a scorching 90 degrees. Thirty-two competitors stood ready to go at the starting line of an exhausting 26.2-mile race. As soon as the race began, things started to go wrong. To begin with, the course had poor signage, which contributed to numerous disoriented racers. Halfway through the marathon, a runner from Cuba named

Felix Carbajal stopped to eat some apples from an orchard. He also made a side trip to a nearby brewery, where he reportedly talked to several spectators and drank some beer. He came in fourth place, but only after being pursued by a pack of wild dogs. Talk about your motivation to run fast.

William Garcia, a runner from the United States, was chased off the course by a group of wild dogs too. He had to climb a tree to get away from them. If these weren't the same dogs that chased Felix, then there was an alarming number of wild dogs in St. Louis in 1904. William eventually finished in twelfth place, but not before being stung by a swarm of bees.

Then there was American Fred Lorz. For most of the race, Fred held the lead, but at the ninth mile, he began to feel nauseous. He ended up hitching a ride in a passing car for a majority of the race. However, the car broke down. That's what you get for cheating. He had to jog the rest of the way. He was crowned first place, but someone called him out on his joyride, and he was disqualified.

But perhaps the most bizarre story of the 1904 marathon involved the winner, Thomas Hicks of the United States. Hicks led the race at the halfway point but struggled in the heat. His trainers followed him in a car and decided to give him a mix of egg whites and strychnine to help him push through the pain. Strychnine is defined as "a bitter and highly poisonous compound obtained from nux vomica, a spiny southern Asian tree with orange fruit and toxic seeds, and related plants." There were definitely some red flags in that definition. Of course, the word "poisonous" was concerning. The word that really stood out was "vomica" for obvious reasons. At the time, strychnine was a common stimulant used by athletes to improve their performance. It was just quite toxic in high doses. Hicks' trainers gave him several doses of the poison, mixed with brandy, to keep him going. As a result, Hicks started hallucinating and became delirious. He probably started seeing monstrous nux vomica plants chasing him. In the end, he crossed the finish line in first place, but he was barely conscious and had to be carried off the course.

Part 3: The Breakdown

Although the 1904 marathon was a complete mess, there were some interesting consequences. The competition revealed numerous problems with how sporting events were managed. As a result, future marathons were run differently. For instance, the International Olympic Committee began to standardize the length of the race. They also created rules about what types of substances athletes were allowed to use during competitions.

The marathon also had some lasting effects on running as a sport. The weird stories from the 1904 race helped popularize running as a form of entertainment and helped pave the way for later marathons and other endurance competitions. Today, marathons are common sporting events held all over the world that draw thousands of participants and spectators. Have you participated in a marathon lately? Just please stay away from the nux vomica.

CHAPTER 3:
THE SAMURAI SHELL

Part 1: The Fact

Over a thousand years ago in Japan, there were many ways to defend yourself in battle in the world of the samurai. Helmets, masks, chest armor, shoulder guards, sleeves, thigh protection, and shin guards made up a samurai's basic armor. Very cool. There was another piece to this ensemble that you don't see very often in photographs of samurai warriors. It might not look as cool (if samurai cared about looking cool back then), but it helped keep them alive all the same.

This piece of armor is called the *horo*. It's simply a big bag with a balloon-like appearance. Samurai of high rank fastened these bags to their backs to shield themselves from arrows. Lower-ranking samurai also used these bags. However, they were much smaller. Although carrying a giant, bobbing balloon on your back may have looked absurd, this strategy worked and prevented many samurai from certain death.

Part 2: The Story

The *horo* was typically several feet in diameter when completely inflated and was constructed of silk or cotton. The samurai would use a bamboo pipe to blow air into the bag enough to cover their back from head to toe. Because it wasn't airtight, the *horo* would flap in the wind and make a loud rustling noise that would warn the samurai of approaching arrows.

Samurai first started using the *horo* as a defensive shield in Japan during the Kamakura period (1185–1333). This was when samurai usually fought on horseback. The *horo* would shield their backs and sides from arrows fired from behind or to the side as they rode toward their adversaries. The samurai could concentrate on their attack without worrying about being hit by arrows from behind.

The *horo* wasn't used only as a barrier of defense. It was also used to intimidate. Seeing a samurai racing toward you with a giant, billowing balloon on their back must have been pretty frightening. You'd probably think the samurai was twice their real size. The dread element would increase by the loud rustling sound the *horo* made, making the enemy think twice before engaging in battle with what looked like a giant, ferocious tortoise.

As combat moved from horseback to foot during the Muromachi period (1336–1573), the use of the *horo* decreased. The samurai started wearing thicker, more protective armor that could better save them from any stray arrows flying around. The *horo* was even less effective when firearms started being used since they were obviously no match for bullets.

Part 3: The Breakdown

Despite its waning appeal, the *horo* is nevertheless an intriguing and distinctive aspect of samurai history. It's evidence of the samurai's inventiveness and resourcefulness as they were constantly coming up with inventive ways to defend themselves in combat.

Fun fact: Samurai used a variety of creative strategies to defend themselves in battle in addition to the *horo*. They would, for instance, wear long-brimmed metal hats that protected their faces and necks. These hats, known as *jingasa*, were made to fend off sword blows and deflect arrows.

The samurai's devotion to their trade can be seen in how they used the *horo*. They aspired to develop fresh, cutting-edge strategies to assure their survival in conflict rather than being satisfied with depending on conventional ways of defense. The utilization of the *horo* serves as a reminder that sometimes the most unusual solutions are the best ones.

With that in mind, if you're ever on the set of a samurai movie, be sure to ask the director where the samurai's *horo* is! They'll probably look at you like what the heck are you talking about, but all you need to do is persuade them the actor won't look silly doing the super cool fight scene with a bloated bubble on their back.

CHAPTER 4:
IN THE LAP OF PINEAPPLE

Part 1: The Fact

Wealth. That was what the pineapple used to symbolize. Owning a fresh pineapple in 18th-century England was more than simply a method to satisfy your fruit cravings. It was a chance to show off your position as a wealthy member of society. Nothing screamed luxury like a golden, tropical fruit.

Part 2: The Story

Foreign foods always fascinated European people in the 18th century, but the pineapple raised the bar to the extreme. It developed into an obsession because it was so unlike anything anyone had ever seen before. Those who were fortunate enough to have a pineapple in their home fell in love with its spiky shell, golden flesh, and sweetness. Even more intriguing is the thought of how someone discovered pineapples were actually a fruit in the first place. They're pretty prickly on the outside and not exactly the most appetizing thing to look at. It's not like you can just bite into it like an apple. So who decided to cut it open and say, "Hey, there's fruit inside!" We may never know, but it's definitely food for thought.

The craze for pineapples led to some intriguing cultural customs. For instance, you could rent pineapples for special events. You could actually rent a pineapple. It was like the fancy car rental of the 18th century. And if you were fortunate enough to own a pineapple, you would proudly exhibit it in all its glory right in the middle of your table at your party where everyone could see it.

Pineapples were often used as meal decorations or display centerpieces. Their images popped up on all sorts of things like clothing, tableware, and cooking utensils. It was like the pineapple had become high society's unofficial symbol. People were so enamored with pineapples that they would put them on everything they owned. Because they used them as decoration, do you think they went as far as decorating their Christmas trees with pineapples?

These fruits were extremely expensive and scarce in England. The basic explanation for this was they could only be grown in tropical areas, making importation extremely difficult and pricey. This strange obsession didn't last long, though. The pineapple enjoyed a good run, but it wasn't until the invention of steamships that made it possible to send large amounts of pineapples to England.

The fruit became more common, so people stopped obsessing over it. Once it became easy to get, it lost its special status.

Part 3: The Breakdown

Pineapples are no longer a symbol of elegance and prosperity, but that doesn't make them any less fascinating. Here are some interesting pineapple facts you might not know:

- Pineapples are a species of bromeliad, a group of tropical plants. Consider a pineapple as a distant relative of your houseplants.

- Bromelain, an enzyme that digests protein, is found only in pineapples. That's why pineapples are a common component of digestion aids and meat tenderizers.

- Pineapples are a significant source of dietary fiber, manganese, and vitamin C. The next time you're looking for a nutritious snack, choose a pineapple over a bag of chips.

Where would you go if you were to go on a quest to find the modern-day luxury fruit? We're exposed to many fruits in today's society, so it's challenging to single out a fruit that stands out as much as the pineapple did in the past. Maybe the answer is a rare fruit that only grows in a faraway region or one that's not frequently found in supermarkets. Have you ever sampled the sapodilla, hala fruit, rambutan, jackfruit, or durian? These fruits continue to captivate the curious foodies even though they may not have gained widespread popularity because some don't exactly smell like a fruity scented candle. Maybe one day, a new fruit will emerge to become the next pineapple of our time.

Part 4: The Sketch

The entryway bubbled with luxury. An impressive staircase led to the upper floors. Ornate blue and white patterns adorned the walls, and the shining white marble floor reflected the sparkling ceiling. In an equally elegant dress of red satin, Daphne followed the butler, Joseph, deeper into the mansion. She marveled at the colorful frescoes on the walls and the velvet sofas. Passing her reflection in a golden mirror, she caught herself smirking. This might have been the wealthy and eccentric Eloise Pepperidgton's mansion, but at least there weren't any "pineapples," Daphne muttered in disdain, stopping in her tracks.

Entering the parlor room, Daphne noticed hundreds of delicately-painted pineapples on the walls. She even saw pineapples wrapped around golden columns, and the candelabras were shaped like pineapples too. She folded her arms and haughtily eyed a statue of a pineapple holding none other than a pineapple. She thought she was the only one in London prosperous enough to have such things. It looked like Eloise was much wealthier than Daphne had thought. The painting of herself holding a single measly pineapple couldn't compare to the overpowering sense of luxury radiating from all of Eloise's pineapples.

"Oh, hello," a man said, extending his gloved hand to Daphne. "Did you notice all that fog outside? I am appalled at the sight of it."

"Of course I noticed it," Daphne said with wisps of fog trailing from her breath. She glanced at the man and recognized his purple knee-length coat. "Your name is Henry, right?"

"It's Henrietta."

Daphne frowned. "Henrietta is your name?"

"Just kidding, Daphne," Henry chuckled, his top hat wiggling on his head.

Daphne crossed her arms. "Wow. I didn't know that kind of humor existed in this time period." She turned around and held up a hand in front of the butler's face. "Excuse me, Joseph?"

The butler blinked at her hand. "Yes?"

"Are Henry and I the only ones who have arrived so far?"

"Do you see anyone else in the room?" Joseph asked.

Daphne quickly looked around. She tried to ignore the pineapple-shaped rug. "I don't."

"Well, there you go."

Henry walked up to Joseph, fussing with his sleeve cuffs. "Joseph, you are the domicile engineer of this estate, correct?"

"Engineer?" Joseph said, confused.

"I meant, are you the domestic engineer?"

"You mean the butler?"

"Yes."

Daphne rolled her eyes. "Wow, Henrietta. Don't make things more complicated than they need to be. Joseph, where is Eloise? I want to know why she invited me here. Is she selling some of her things?" Daphne picked up a goblet shaped like a pineapple. She could use that in her dining room. Making sure no one was looking, she stuffed the goblet into the folds of her gown.

"Eloise is detained," Joseph informed the guests. "Detained by lions."

"Isn't this her party?" Henry asked.

"Yes. She will come out of her mundane existence shortly."

Henry watched Joseph walk away and whispered to Daphne, "That was strange. I bet the butler did it, whatever it is."

"I'm strange," Daphne said absentmindedly. "They call me Daphne Strange."

"Isn't this mansion just brilliant, Daphne?" Henry asked, looking around. He ran his fingers over a chair embroidered with tiny pineapples. "I love the decor."

Daphne shrugged. "It's nice if you like contemporary tropical." She eyed a row of pineapple-shaped vases on a shelf above the fireplace. She wanted those vases too. She wanted everything pineapple-themed in that room for her own mansion, anything to prove herself superior to insufferable Eloise. She wondered if Eloise had actual pineapples to eat. Daphne rented a pineapple for her own party once, but it turned rotten before the guests arrived. She would have rented another pineapple if it hadn't cost so much.

"Look at this!" Henry exclaimed, pointing at a door handle shaped like a pineapple. "Eloise must be incredibly wealthy. She's probably traveled the world on many seafaring adventures."

"Wow, what a seafarer," Daphne exhaled.

"I wonder who else is attending this pineapple party?" Henry said.

"I have no idea," Daphne replied.

Just then, the doors opened. Joseph walked in with a couple behind him. He motioned for them to join Henry and Daphne.

"Oh, look!" Henry said, waving. "It's Sir Uh and Jane."

The younger woman, dressed in a pale blue gown imprinted with flowers, pointed to herself. "I'm Jane. Who's Sara?"

"Sir Uh," the man beside her said, clearing his throat. "I'm Sir Uh."

"Do you think I said 'Sara?'" Henry asked.

Jane pointed to her giant hat with an equally giant feather in it. "Sorry if this hat slips over my ears, preventing me from hearing properly."

Sir Uh took one look at the room through his monocle and whistled. "Our hostess must be very wealthy to have so many depictions of the pineapple throughout her home. I'm not wealthy enough to have even one picture."

"Can't you draw one on a pillow or something?" Jane asked.

"I can't draw. Also, I can't write."

"I've never seen a real pineapple in person," Jane tittered. "Do you think Eloise will have a live pineapple for us to sample tonight?"

Daphne bit her lip. "I hope not. It would be like a slap in the face to me, who couldn't even rent one properly."

Jane sighed dreamily. "What do you think a pineapple actually smells and tastes like?"

Henry shrugged. "I don't know, but I dream about it sometimes. Daphne, you've tasted pineapple before. Tell them what it tastes like."

"You've tasted pineapple?" Jane cried. "No way!"

"I have," Daphne said, her lip curling into a proud smirk. "I didn't eat the one I rented because it went bad, but I did have the luxury of owning one once before dropping it down a well." She smiled, hoping to impress the others. The smile quickly faded. For some reason, she couldn't remember what that pineapple tasted like. "Um, well… it's called a pineapple, so obviously it tastes like a combination of an apple and pine leaves. Why else would they have called it a pineapple?"

"I've never had an apple," Jane said. "I have eaten pine leaves, though. Don't ask me why."

"More guests are arriving," the butler announced in the doorway. He stepped aside to make room for two women in overflowing white gowns. He disappeared for a second in the folds until the women walked past him. "Presenting Lady Pamela and her stepdaughter, Sophronia."

"So-whata?" Daphne blubbered.

"Sophronia," the younger woman blurted. "Why are you acting like you've never heard that name before?"

"Where is Eloise?" Lady Pamela asked in a wheezy voice. She held up a pair of half-moon spectacles and looked around. "Is Eloise here? I don't see her. My goodness, by the looks of these pineapples, her wealth has no bounds."

"We don't know where Eloise is," Henry said. "We haven't seen her yet."

"She's been detained by a lion, apparently," Daphne added.

"May I have your attention!" Joseph announced. He stood in the middle of the doorway to the parlor room, sandwiched between two golden pineapple columns. "May I introduce your hostess for the evening, Eloise Pepperidgton, the wealthiest woman in all of England!"

Daphne almost choked.

As Joseph stepped aside, Eloise made her grand entrance. Gasps of awe filled the room as Eloise sauntered in. Her white gown sparkled with intricately painted pineapples and trailed behind her on the floor, and pineapples covered her elbow-length gloves. Her hair was fashioned in the shape of a pineapple with leafy points rising toward the sky.

"Hello, guests," Eloise said smugly, flashing a bright smile. "Do you like my ensemble?"

"I love your dress, Eloise!" Sophronia exclaimed. "I'm literally about to take it from you."

"Please don't rip my dress off me," Eloise snapped.

"Yeah, I know. Who knows what color underpants you're wearing. Have underpants been invented yet?"

Daphne glowered at the tropical sight. Why hadn't she ever thought of creating a pineapple dress? That was the ultimate stamp of luxuriousness. She too wanted to rip that dress off Eloise and run away with it into the night.

"I wish I was you," Sophronia was saying.

"I know," Eloise tittered. "Everyone does. Anyway, thank you all for coming to my party. You're all in for a treat." She held out her hand, and Joseph stepped around her to place a beautifully fresh pineapple in it. Everyone stared at it. Even Daphne couldn't take her eyes off it. "We're going to have pineapple pork, pineapple lamb, pineapple potatoes, pineapple beans, pineapple shellfish, and pineapple baked goods!"

Henry winced. "Not sure if that sounds appetizing or not."

"Everything has pineapple in it?" Jane gushed. "You are so better than us by default."

"Will there be any pineapple-themed games?" Henry wondered.

"Yes," Eloise said. "Pin the Tail on the Pineapple."

"How do you pin a tail on a pineapple?" Sophronia asked. "Is it a real tail?"

"We have a bunch of rats in the basement," Eloise replied.

Daphne stepped forward. "Can I, um, hold it?" She had every intention of grabbing that pineapple and running home to drown it in saltwater to keep it from rotting.

"No," Eloise snapped, pulling the pineapple away. "Before we eat, I have something to tell you all. I've called you all here today because you are my closest friends."

"I've never met you before in my life," Sophronia said.

"And I've decided," Eloise continued, "to give one of you every single one of my hundreds of pineapples."

Daphne dropped the pineapple spoon she was in the process of smuggling into her gown. "Excuse me?" She wanted those pineapples. She had to have them. She'd be the wealthiest person in all of England!

"I've thought about giving some to each and every one of you," Eloise said, "but I just decided right now to give them all to one person and one person only."

"Please me," Daphne breathed.

Eloise held her pineapple out in front of her. "I am giving all of my pineapples to my dearly devoted butler, Joseph."

"Joseph?" Daphne thundered.

"Is there a love affair going on?" Jane asked.

"More than that," Eloise said cryptically.

"You have a kid together?"

"More than that."

"What's more than that?"

Eloise handed the pineapple to an awestruck Joseph. "We just like each other as friends."

"So the rest of us don't get any pineapples?" Henry clarified.

"That's correct," Eloise stated with a nod, her pineapple hair bobbing along with her. "But I'm giving the rest of you some money."

Daphne's mouth fell open. "I don't want your money! I want your pineapples!" She pushed past Henry and lunged at Eloise, catching her off guard. "Give me your pineapple!" Daphne grabbed Eloise's pineapple gown and yanked as hard as she could. "Give me your dress!"

"She's gone mad!" Sir Uh cried out.

"What do you expect from a girl named Daphne Strange?" Henry yelped.

"Triumph!" Daphne shouted, standing up with Eloise's gown in her arms.

On the floor, Eloise extended her hand to Joseph. "It's a good thing I'm wearing my pineapple underpants. Joseph, take me upstairs. I'm going to immerse myself in my final pineapple juice bath."

"I have the pineapple gown!" Daphne declared in a hysterical hiss, her eyes darting back and forth frantically. "I am all-powerful! Now I just need the pineapples. Joseph, where are they?"

Joseph looked up from dragging Eloise along the floor and gulped nervously. "Uh, they're in the pantry."

"Yes!" Daphne exclaimed, leaving the parlor and rushing into the kitchen with the voluminous gown still in her arms. She forced her way into the pantry and fell to her knees at the sight of rows upon rows of stunning golden pineapples. "Yes! I am now the wealthiest person in all of England!"

Daphne's hysterical screams drowned out a faint clicking sound from outside the pantry. On the other side of the door, Joseph held up a key and dropped it into Eloise's outstretched hand. "She's locked in the pantry, as you wished."

Eloise smirked and smiled wickedly. "Excellent. With Daphne finally out of the way, no one can come close to surpassing my wealth. I will forever be the wealthiest in all of England!"

Joseph nervously pointed to the pantry door. "But how will you get your pineapples to show anyone if you turned your pantry into a cage?"

Eloise looked at Joseph's pineapple he was still cradling in his arms. "A pineapple is a fruit. A fruit has seeds. Seeds are meant to be planted. Henceforth, we can grow as many pineapples as we want in my greenhouse. Honestly, why no one's figured that out yet and is so gaga over just seeing a pineapple makes no sense to me."

CHAPTER 5:
KILROY WAS HERE

Part 1: The Fact

It's a well-known graffiti tagline that's puzzled historians, enchanted troops, and perplexed alley cats for generations. How did it get started? Who came up with it? Most importantly, why did the big-nosed man need to shove his sniffer over a wall? Introducing Kilroy. He isn't a who but a what. The simple drawing, typically seen in graffiti, depicts a bald man with an unusually long nose peeking over a wall with both hands gripping the top like he trying to climb over it. The meme popped up everywhere during World War II. No one knows where it came from.

Part 2: The Story

Although Kilroy's beginnings remain a mystery, we do know that he was here, as clearly stated by the words "Kilroy Was Here," that typically accompanied the drawing. Some say he was a shipyard inspector, a railroad worker, or a soldier. Whatever his line of work, one thing was certain: Kilroy was everywhere.

Soldiers stationed all around the world during World War II found Kilroy's slogan and doodle in the most unexpected places. They discovered him on vehicles, structures, and even in hostile areas. The phrase "Kilroy Was Here" became a common way for soldiers to show they had been there first and leave their mark on history.

But more than just the phrase gained popularity. It was the accompanying doodle. Kilroy was always portrayed as a bald man with a large nose who peered over a wall while holding on to it. The picture was straightforward, but it was quite clear. It served as a calling card for soldiers, allowing them to quickly and simply state they were present.

Not only troops had a soft spot for Kilroy. People back home joined in on the fun as well. They started printing Kilroy's picture on everything, including postcards, coffee cups, and t-shirts. He was sort of like a celebrity, but instead of paparazzi following him around, it was just soldiers with cans of spray paint.

Part 3: The Breakdown

What was the point of this meme? Was Kilroy simply a joke made by troops to pass the time? Maybe. But there was also a more profound significance at play. During a period when the nation was at war, Kilroy represented the American spirit. He stood for the notion that, no matter where you were in the world, someone else was looking out for you. Kilroy served as a constant reminder that there was hope even in the worst circumstances.

Kilroy teaches us that even the most basic things can

have a significant impact. Kilroy's slogan and doodle weren't particularly creative or required any art degrees to make, yet they struck a chord with the public in a way no one could have anticipated. We can also learn that using comedy as a strategy in difficult circumstances can be effective. Kilroy was crucial in injecting some lightheartedness into a dire circumstance.

Kilroy teaches us that there's always a reason to keep going, regardless of what is happening in the world. This is possibly the most significant lesson we can take away from him. There's always a reason to press on, despite any obstacles you may be experiencing. Perhaps someone in the future will come across your mark on history and wonder who you were and what you stood for. So go out there and be like Kilroy. Just don't do what he's doing because no one wants to see you rubbing your nose on everything.

CHAPTER 6:
THE ORDER OF THE PUG

Part 1: The Fact

There have been some incredibly unusual organizations in the history of secret societies, but probably none as bizarre as the Order of the Pug. This exclusive club was founded in Bavaria around 1740 by a group of Roman Catholics who wanted to establish a para-Masonic organization, because founding a para-Masonic society was on everybody's bucket list. They also wanted a distinctive name for their group. Naming themselves "The Secret Society" was apparently already taken. These men wanted a name that would truly distinguish them from other underground organizations even though it was created to be a secret group, so no one else should have even known about them in the first place.

Part 2: The Story

The Order of the Pug is definitely a distinctive name. In the 18th century, pugs were a popular breed, distinguished by their wrinkled faces and adorable snorting sounds. The pug was also a symbol of society. The group's followers thought they had qualities in common with these obedient dogs: courage, loyalty, and determination. These were all traits the Order highly valued. Therefore, they decided that everyone in the Order would take on the persona of a pug-literally.

In order to join the club, new members had to go through a somewhat humiliating initiation rite. To gain entry, they had to put on a dog collar and scratch at the door to be let in. It's not clear if there was any barking involved. That'd be borderline disturbing. Once inside, the Order of the Pug members would partake in a variety of secret tasks. Of course there were ceremonies, secret handshakes or maybe pawshakes, and passwords. Members were also expected to protect the group's secrets at all costs and to have the utmost loyalty to the group. It looks like someone blabbed because otherwise, this chapter would be blank.

The Order of the Pug was supposedly highly active for many years despite its somewhat absurd beginnings. It even managed to attract some high-profile people like Franz Joseph Haydn, a well-known classical composer. However, the Order started to disappear by the turn of the 20th century. Although it was formally disbanded in 1902, its legacy lives on in a small number of remaining artifacts and records.

Part 3: The Breakdown

The odd story of the Order of the Pug serves as a reminder that secret societies have existed for a very long time and that the appeal of exclusivity and secrecy has always attracted people. It serves as a reminder that even the most serious and secret of groups occasionally have a sense of humor too. The ability of silly and playfulness, even in the middle of serious tasks, can be seen in the members of the Order of the Pug's willingness to dress up like dogs and scratch at doors.

There's also something to be said about how the Order of the Pug brought people together around a shared interest. The members of the Order managed to bond with one another and create a community, whether it was via their shared love of pugs or their desire to join a secret club. In today's world where many of us occasionally feel detached and lonely, there's something exciting about the concept of a bunch of people joining together around a similar goal, even if that goal is as silly as pretending to be a dog.

The Order of the Pug's tale is a fun and cheerful reminder of the amazing and bizarre things people are capable of. Maybe someday we'll see the rise of another bizarre secret society with its own unique rituals and traditions. Maybe they'll all wear cat ears and meow to gain entry, or perhaps they'll dress up as moon-loving beavers. We can be certain it'll be just as absurd, silly, and interesting as the Order of the Pug in whatever shape it takes.

CHAPTER 7:
GOLDFISH DOWN

Part 1: The Fact

We've already dabbled in the 1930s a bit with the mention of the mongoose poltergeist, the Dymaxion car, and the dictionary mishap, but of course there are more weird happenings in this decade we can't leave out. The 1930s is also known as the time when the fad of goldfish swallowing began.

Part 2: The Story

As weird as it may sound, college campuses across the United States were swept up in the trend of swallowing live goldfish whole. Well, it was the time of the Great Depression, and people didn't have a lot to laugh about at the time, so this was apparently a way to add some fun to their lives. They surely could have found something else to laugh at, like, literally anything else. So how did this odd craze even start, and what made it so popular?

Believe it or not, the origins of the trend can be traced back to Harvard University. Students were at an on-campus party, and someone apparently suggested they each swallow a live goldfish to add some life to the party. That must have been a really dull party to suggest such a thing. Although it's unclear if anyone actually did swallow any live goldfish that night, the idea quickly spread. Before long, other colleges joined in. The practice of goldfish swallowing quickly became a full-out fad.

The question is, why goldfish? It turns out that goldfish were affordable and simple to find, especially at a time when people had a lot of financial difficulties. Plus, they were small enough to swallow whole. This couldn't have been comfortable for either party. In fact, some students even started swallowing multiple goldfish at once.

As you can expect, not everyone was too thrilled with this new trend. Understandably upset, animal rights campaigners demanded a halt to the practice. However, selling live goldfish as carnival prizes was still allowed at the time, so they couldn't do much about it. The United States didn't start passing legislation to outlaw the sale of live animals as prizes until the 1940s, effectively putting an end to goldfish swallowing.

Part 3: The Breakdown

It's interesting to consider the cultural and societal elements that might have influenced goldfish swallowing. It's possible that goldfish swallowing was a means for young people to rebel against the severe social conventions of the time during the 1930s, a period of economic hardship and social upheaval. It also provided an opportunity for friendship and fun in an otherwise depressing world.

Naturally, we can't discuss goldfish swallowing without bringing up the obvious similarities to the modern world. Thankfully, we're no longer dropping pet fish down our throats, but we're still experiencing our own share of strange and unusual trends. However, there might be something useful to take away from goldfish swallowing. It's a reminder that just because something is fun or trendy doesn't necessarily mean it's okay to do, regardless of how ridiculous and innocent it may seem at the time. We need to be aware of the effects our actions have on the world around us.

In the end, goldfish swallowing may have been an odd and brief fad, but it nevertheless played a role in shaping our culture. People in the future will most likely reflect on our own bizarre fads and wonder what we were thinking. All we can do is try to have a little fun without harming anyone or any innocent goldfish.

CHAPTER 8:
THE GLASS DELUSION

Part 1: The Fact

Some people in the Middle Ages had this crazy delusion they were made of glass. Yes, glass. People thought they had glass skin, not flesh or bone but a material that could easily break with a single tap.

Part 2: The Story

This delusion, aptly named the glass delusion, afflicted an unusual number of people from the 15th to 17th centuries. This happened in the Middle Ages? More like the Dumb Ages. It was like people were hit with the sudden desire to be fragile and reflective. These individuals believed they would shatter into a million pieces like a broken vase if they moved the wrong way. We've all had our clumsy moments, but imagine being afraid of breaking yourself just by walking around. That was some next-level paranoia.

Let's take a closer look at two shining examples of this glass delusion. King Charles VI, a ruler of France, demanded that iron rods be sewn into his clothes to prevent himself from shattering if he touched someone else. He thought he was so fragile that even a slight bump would turn him into a pile of glass shards.

Then there was Princess Alexandra Amalie of Bavaria. Her glass delusion was a bit different. She claimed to have swallowed a grand piano as a child and was terrified of shattering it inside her stomach and puncturing her intestines. Now, this statement brings up a lot of questions. How does one swallow a piano? Was it a mini piano or a full-sized one? How did it fit down her esophagus? Did she swallow it key by key? If swallowing a grand piano was actually possible, then why did she even do it in the first place? Princess Alexandra Amalie didn't exactly think this story through too well.

Part 3: The Breakdown

The idea of having glass skin may seem like a bizarre and far-fetched concept to us today, but it was a very real concern for some people in the past. The glass delusion, which primarily affected nobles and scholars, was likely caused by a fixation on glass, a pretty luxurious material during the Middle Ages and rare to come by. It was something only wealthier people, like nobles or scholars, could afford. So the smarter you were supposed to be, the higher your chance of believing in such a dumb thing was? Maybe, or maybe not. Fixation on a luxurious material perhaps could have manifested the notion that because people like nobles and scholars lived luxuriously, they therefore were made of a luxurious material.

Thankfully, records of any new cases of people thinking they were made of glass stopped after the mid-1800s. What changed their minds? Probably because nobody actually shattered.

It's fascinating to think about what other strange beliefs we might have today that future generations will look back on with amusement. So let's raise a glass to our glassy predecessors and be thankful that we no longer have to live in fear of shattering into a million pieces. However, even if we did think that, at least we'd have the modern technologies of bubble wrap and cotton balls to wrap ourselves in.

Part 4: The Sketch

Beatrice shuffled down the dimly lit hallway, her hand tracing the rough stones of the wall as she went. Her goal for the morning was simply to reach the front door and step outside. It had taken her nearly two hours to crawl out of her straw bed and dress herself with her cumbersome floor-length tunic. She hoped she didn't trip. She didn't want to break herself.

"Steady," Beatrice muttered to herself, stepping over a clump of dirt. "You cannot bump into a thing. Oh no!" She felt her big toe brush against the edge of the hearth. She hesitantly lifted her dress, fearing the worst. Upon seeing her bare foot, she sighed with relief. *Oh, thank goodness. I didn't shatter.*

She wiggled her toe. It was fully intact. *That was close. That could have been shattertastic. I'd hate to walk around with one less toe even though with these impossible gowns, no one can even see my toes.*

Beatrice let her gown fall back to the floor. She eyed the door, determined to reach it before the morning passed. *But I have to be careful. I'm made out of glass, after all.*

After what felt like an eternity of shuffling through the dirt and around the hay in the livestock corner where her angry cow stood mooing all day long, she finally found herself at the front door. "About time. Hello, good morning! Ah!" Someone thrust the door open in her face from the outside before she could open it, knocking her backward.

"Hey, Beatrice! It's me, Roger!" A friendly face half-hidden by a mangy straw hat peeked inside. "Remember me?"

"Yes!" Beatrice shouted, steadying herself. She held her arms out to either side.

Roger just stared at her. "What are you doing?"

"Balancing myself."

"Is that what you've been doing all morning?"

"What do you want, Roger?" Beatrice snapped, quietly counting her fingers to make sure none had broken off.

Roger stepped inside and kicked aside some hay. "I just wanted to say hey." He reached out to give her a friendly hug.

"Don't touch me!" Beatrice screeched fearfully.

Roger jumped and recoiled. His expression changed from confusion to alarm. "What?"

"I'm made out of glass!" Beatrice cried in exasperation as she wrapped her arms around herself.

Roger blinked in confusion. "Excuse me?"

Beatrice huffed, really not wanting to repeat herself. "I'm made out of glass. I just decided that today, and I believe it. See for yourself." Beatrice held out her bare arm for emphasis.

Roger leaned forward and inspected her arm. Apart from the unusually bulbous veins, it looked completely normal. "Uh, it looks pretty fleshy to me."

"That shows how much you know, Roger. I literally woke up this morning and was like, 'Whoa, I'm made of glass.' It just hit me. I mean, how did I not ever realize it?"

"It just hit you?" Roger asked.

"Yes."

"Then why didn't you shatter?"

Beatrice frowned. "Well, I was on my bed around a bunch of fluffy pillows, which was lucky because then I would have shattered, and you'd be talking to me all over the floor."

Roger folded his arms. He didn't look too convinced about Beatrice's story. "I feel like you're making this all up as you go along. You really think you're made of glass?"

"Of course not," Beatrice said, rolling her eyes. "I *know* I'm made of glass."

"Have you been talking to Princess Alexandra?"

Beatrice cleared her throat nervously. "Maybe."

"Well, that's dumb," Roger informed her.

"Dumb?"

"Well, this is the Middle Ages. We're all dumb by default. I'm convinced brown cows make chocolate milk, but that's another story."

"I know of other things that are by default," Beatrice said quickly. She wanted to change the subject. The fact that Roger apparently didn't believe her was starting to get on her nerves.

"Like what?"

"Like, um, salad."

Roger shook his head. "I don't think salad is a thing yet. We just eat grass."

"Oh yeah. Then I meant bowls."

"I don't think bowls are a thing yet, either."

"Yes, they are. Now if you please…" Beatrice held her arms out and motioned for Roger to step away from the door. "I'd like to get some fresh air. Living with my livestock is beginning to put a real damper on things. It isn't raining out, is it? Or a better question yet is, it isn't hailing out, is it? I'd break for sure if a storm of hail rained down upon me."

Roger shook his head again. "Beatrice, you're not made of glass."

"Yes, I am," Beatrice trilled, shooting an annoyed glance at Roger. "I can hear myself clinking. Either my teeth are chattering because it's really cold in here, or I'm made of glass. The latter makes much more sense."

Roger leaned forward into Beatrice's face. "Wouldn't I see my reflection in your face if you were glass?"

"What, you don't see your reflection in my face?" Beatrice asked.

"No, I just see your face."

"How do you know that's not *your* face, and we just look alike?"

Roger stared blankly at her. "Okay, I'm going to push you now to prove you're not made of glass."

"Don't push me!" Beatrice screamed at the top of her lungs. She shut her eyes and braced herself. "Are you going to push me?"

"No. The ground is filthy. You'd look like you were made of mud instead, and that's worse than glass."

The door burst open again, and Beatrice's neighbors, Amabel and Lucan, barreled in. They nearly pushed Roger over into the dirt floor.

"Watch it!" Roger shouted.

"Hey, Beatrice!" Amabel cried, waving her hands frantically. "I haven't seen you all morning. I was beginning to think you forgot to wake up. I tend to do that myself."

Beatrice winced at Amabel's high-pitched voice. "Hi, Amabel. Can you do me a favor and lower your volume? Your sound waves could shatter me. Not that I know what sound waves are since I'm here in the Middle Ages where we're all dumb."

"Shatter you?" Lucan asked, raising an eyebrow. "What does that mean?"

"I'm made of glass, duh," Beatrice said as if it was obvious.

"Yeah," Roger sighed. "Beatrice thinks she's made of glass."

"You're made of glass?" Amabel said in awe. Her eyes widened like she had never heard of such a thing. "Wait. What's glass? I haven't had the pleasure of experiencing this anonymity."

"It's the stuff you see in church windows," Lucan explained to her.

"Church?" Amabel repeated idly.

Lucan rolled his eyes. "Yes. Good job."

"Can I touch you, Beatrice?" Amabel asked. "That sounded weird."

"Ever so gently," Beatrice quipped, extending her arm again.

"Wow," Amabel said while sliding her finger along Beatrice's arm. "Your skin is so fragile and slippery."

"Don't encourage her, Amabel," Roger snapped. "Look, Beatrice. Why do you think you're made of glass in the first place?"

Beatrice thought for a moment. "Um, what do you mean by that question?"

"I mean, why do you think you're made of glass in the first place?"

"Oh. Thank you for that clarification. Well, because I woke up today and was reminded I was made of glass. The heavens came down to me in a vision."

"You're holy!" Amabel cried.

"I better not be," Beatrice said, inspecting her arm for any holes.

"Well, this has been fun," Lucan whistled, "but Amabel and I came over to ask you guys if you wanted to do something together."

"We could wrestle," Roger said, eyeing Beatrice. "Want to wrestle, Beatrice?"

"Uh, no."

"Why the heck not?"

"Forgive me for not just wanting to wrestle."

"How about some hammer-throwing?" Lucan suggested. "It's a great day for it!"

"I love hammer-throwing," Roger said excitedly, bouncing on the balls of his bare feet. "I'm the hammer-throwing champ around here. I can throw a hammer farther than anyone!"

"Why do you sound so proud of that?" Beatrice mumbled.

"I have some hammers right here all ready for us," Lucan said, taking a heavy hammer from a knapsack.

Beatrice took one look at the hammer and screamed. "Get it away from me, the foul thing!" She held her hands up over her face in fear.

"Calm down, Beatrice," Lucan said, lowering the hammer. "I'm not going to throw it at you."

"Oh good." Beatrice instantly calmed down and lowered her hands. "I don't think I can play, though. I'd probably break if I put too much effort into things like hammer-throwing."

"No, I think you should play," Roger said teasingly. "If you throw the hammer and you shatter, then you'll know you're made out of glass for sure. But if you don't shatter, then you're not glass, and you can get on with your life and do your chores. Hey, is this whole glass thing a ruse to get out of milking your cow-"

"Throw the hammer, Roger!" Beatrice shouted rather sharply. "Go on, throw it!"

"Watch this." Roger snatched the hammer from Lucan's hand and raised his arm back. With a snap of his wrist, he threw it as hard as he could. He grinned as the hammer sailed right through the thatch roof, leaving behind a giant hole. "Wasn't that amazing?"

Beatrice glared at him. "Could you maybe not destroy my house, which already looks destroyed since it was built in the Middle Ages?"

"My turn!" Amabel yelped. She grabbed a hammer out of Lucan's knapsack. With a wobbly twirl and a few overly-exaggerated jabs in the air, she let the hammer fly. "Did I throw it far?"

Lucan pointed at her feet. "You just dropped it."

"Oh. Drats."

"What even was that?" Beatrice asked Amabel. "You looked like a quail."

"A quail?"

"A pudgy little bird."

"What about it?"

"You looked like one."

Amabel beamed. "Oh, thanks!"

"My turn," Lucan said, holding up a hammer. "I think I'll throw it… this way…" He slowly turned toward Beatrice.

"No!" Beatrice screamed. She closed her eyes again. "Please, no! Why do you want to see me break into a million pieces?"

Lucan lowered the hammer. "Okay, this is ridiculous. Beatrice, you're not made of glass."

"I'm made of bread," Amabel trumpeted.

Everyone looked at her.

Amabel nodded feverishly. "Yep. Bread. I have some tasty buns."

Roger slapped his hand over his face in despair. "This is maddening."

"Finally, a sympathizer," Beatrice spluttered, patting Amabel on the shoulder. "One who understands the woes of being something other than flesh and blood. Ew. I just realized, If I'm made of glass, is there no blood inside me then? That's weird."

"There's butter inside me," Amabel said, licking her lips. "I sound so good right now."

"If you're made of bread," Lucan said, "how did you lift that hammer?"

Amabel looked at the hammer at her feet. "I'm made of very strong flour mixed with the purest of wheat."

Beatrice noticed Roger looking at her strangely. "What, Roger?"

"I was just thinking. Beatrice, if you're made of glass, how can you go to work? You're a jongleur."

Beatrice bit her lip in thought. For some reason, she had never heard that word before. She didn't want Roger to know that, though. "Uh, yes. Of course I am. It's one of the best professions in the Middle Ages. Remind me what it is so I can tell my mom I got a job."

"You assist the troubadour," Roger explained.

Beatrice nodded slowly. "Yes. The troubadour, I assist."

"You assist him by juggling in his shows."

"I'm a joker?" Beatrice cried.

Roger laughed. "No! You're a juggler. You juggle behind the troubadour while he sings during his shows. How can you juggle those heavy items if you're made of glass?"

"Good question," Beatrice said thoughtfully.

"That's why I asked it," Roger snapped.

Beatrice shrugged. "Well, I plan on replacing those lead balls that are in no way at all toxic with soft and squishy cotton balls."

Roger threw his hands up in defeat. "Okay, I give up. Since you're so utterly convinced you're made of glass, you just make no sense to any of us. You're just going to have to deal with living like that on your own. Just know you're living a lie."

Beatrice's lips turned into an angry thin line. She really wanted to stomp her foot in her anger but decided not to since her foot would shatter. "Oh yeah? Well, you're the one who's living a lie for telling me I'm living a lie!"

"Okay, I'm leaving." Roger slipped through the front door.

"Same," Lucan said, shouldering his knapsack. He turned to Amabel and asked, "Coming, loaf? Hey, I'm hungry."

Amabel gasped. "Don't eat me!" She took off running and ran right past Beatrice's cow in the livestock corner. Startled, the cow jumped in fright and took off running.

Beatrice spun around and saw the cow running straight for her. "No! I'm too young to shatter! Oomph!" The cow rammed into her stomach. Beatrice fell onto her back and screamed as part of the roof caved in on her. She just knew she shattered. She just knew it. "I am broken," she said weakly, spitting out hay. "So broken. Somebody pick up my pieces!" She inspected herself and was surprised to find herself in one piece. "Oh. Was I not made out of glass after all?" She wiggled her toes. "If I didn't break, I must be softer than I thought. Oh no! I'm not made of glass. I'm made of hay!"

CHAPTER 9:
REDHEADED VAMPIRES

Part 1: The Fact

Redheads have been the subject of fascination and myths for centuries. From associations with witches in medieval Europe to stereotypes as hotheaded in modern times, redheads have had their fair share of craziness. One of the strangest myths about redheads comes from ancient Greece, when people believed they were vampires.

Part 2: The Story

Typical for living in the Mediterranean climate, the average ancient Greek had black hair, dark eyes, and light to moderately tan skin. Redheads, on the other hand, looked a little different. They had extremely fair, pale skin that of course made them sensitive to the sun. This made them stand out and become the subject of scrutiny. People thought redheads had a thirst for blood and were immortal. It wasn't a rare sight for people to accuse redheads of being vampires and spreading diseases.

The myth of redheads being vampires in ancient Greece can be traced back to the story of Lamia, a woman who was turned into a child-eating monster by the goddess Hera. According to the myth, Hera became enraged after discovering Lamia had an affair with her husband, Zeus. Hera kidnapped and killed Lamia's children in revenge. A strongly-worded note would have done just fine, Hera. As a result, Lamia went understandably insane. However, her insanity drove her to devour any child she came across. These gruesome acts caused Lamia to transform into a hideous monster. That monster was described as having pale skin and red hair, which may have contributed to the association of redheads with vampirism.

It goes without saying that being a redhead in ancient Greece must not have been very fun. Taking pleasant walks down the cobblestone street must have included several acts of ducking behind olive trees or pretending to be statues to get away from people screaming at them. At least headscarves were a common accessory at the time, so redheads could hide their hair if they wanted to. Of course, this didn't completely protect them from discrimination and persecution. A head scarf could only do so much.

Part 3: The Breakdown

The myth that redheads were vampires lingered in ancient Greece for centuries despite being absolutely ridiculous. The myth didn't start to disappear until the spread of Christianity. Then the concept of the vampire became associated with Satan and was considered a sin, which led to the gradual decline of vampire folklore in Greece.

The belief that redheads were vampires in ancient Greece is an example of how people can fear and discriminate against those who are different. Redheads were the subject of stories and distrust because of how distinctive they looked. In today's world, we still see instances of discrimination against people who are different. People typically have a fear of the unknown, and this dread frequently results in prejudice and discrimination. We must learn to appreciate and celebrate diversity rather than fear it. Only then can we truly create an accepting and inclusive world for all.

CHAPTER 10:
LAWN CHAIR LARRY

Part 1: The Fact

Larry Walters was a man with a simple dream. He wanted to fly. Simple, right? He was determined to make that dream a reality. In 1982, he set out to accomplish this dream with some very practical equipment: a lawn chair and 42 helium balloons.

Part 2: The Story

Larry had a plan. He would stock up on supplies, tie 42 weather balloons to his lawn chair, take a seat, and then fly up into the sky. Because nothing could go wrong in that scenario, right? Larry had all the angles planned out so that nothing would go wrong. He secured himself to his chair with a few cords so that he wouldn't drift away into nothingness, and in case he needed to descend rapidly, he brought along a pellet gun so he could fire the balloons one by one.

On July 2, 1982, Larry cut the tethers, sat down in his lawn chair, and started to drift upward. His strategy involved rising to around 100 feet before floating slowly over the Mojave Desert. However, things didn't quite go according to plan. Larry's first problem was that the balloons didn't take him up to 100 feet. They took him up just a little bit higher to something like 16,000 feet. Yikes! He was basically on the moon with those beavers.

Thankfully, Larry started to realize he was in danger as he floated higher and higher, especially since the temperature started to drop. The lack of oxygen at that altitude also made it hard for him to breathe. The helium in those balloons wasn't going to help him with that. At this point, he would have been better off flying in an airplane to the Mohave Desert.

Larry started to shoot some of the balloons down as he floated along in an effort to descend. Disaster then struck. He accidentally dropped his pellet gun. He couldn't control his descent without it. He eventually ended up drifting into the airspace of Los Angeles International Airport. The air traffic controllers were not amused.

Fortunately, Larry avoided any incoming airplanes and ended up landing in a neighborhood in Long Beach, California. The fire department had to save him when he became caught in some power cables. He was detained by the police as soon as he touched down for invading airspace. Despite this, Larry quickly rose to fame and shared his tale on numerous talk shows.

Part 3: The Breakdown

Larry's unusual adventure demonstrated that everything is possible if you put enough effort and creativity into it. Even if it meant jeopardizing his life, Larry was prepared to do whatever it took to realize his lifelong dream. It demonstrated the value of preparation as well. Even though Larry had carefully planned his adventure, he nevertheless ran into unforeseen difficulties. He had no other options after dropping his pellet gun, which was his only method of controlling his descent. In today's world, where we frequently confront unforeseen difficulties and emergencies, it's crucial to have a backup plan in place.

This little high-flying adventure also serves as a reminder that sometimes our dreams may not be the safest or most sensible things to do. While Larry's experience was amusing, it also put him in grave danger. Any endeavor should be carefully planned out before starting, especially if it involves potentially hazardous actions.

Lawn Chair Larry's bizarre and amazing lawn chair flight captivated the interest of people all around the world. Even though his techniques were a little unconventional, his tenacity, ingenuity, and spirit of adventure inspired many. Although we might not all be able to fly away on a lawn chair, we can still take something away from Larry's experience and apply it to our own lives. Larry's legacy is a testament to the strength of aspiration and willpower. So, the next time you find yourself dreaming of doing something crazy, remember Lawn Chair Larry and his incredible flight. You may be inspired to reach for the skies in your own unique way. Or you can participate in the aviation sport called Cluster Ballooning. It's a type of ballooning where a harness attaches a person to a cluster of helium-inflated rubber balloons. Yes, it's a thing.

CHAPTER 11:
THE HORSE THE SENATOR

Part 1: The Fact

A strange emperor by the name of Gaius once lived in the Roman Empire. He was nicknamed Caligula, which is Latin for "little boots." The name might have been a tribute to his military experience, but it also suggested he was a bit of a small guy, both in stature and mind with an emphasis on the mind. During his brief reign from 37 to 41 AD, Caligula, a peculiar and unpredictable ruler, did many strange things. One of his most infamous acts was making his favorite horse, Incitatus, a senator. You might think Caligula did this as a joke, but he was quite serious.

Part 2: The Story

Incitatus was not any ordinary horse. He was a magnificent white stallion with a sleek coat and graceful gait. Caligula loved him dearly and pampered him with all sorts of lavish things. For example, Incitatus had a marble stall with heated flooring, an ivory feeding trough with the best oats and hay, and a sparkling jeweled collar. But it didn't end there. Caligula built a special house for Incitatus that included a stable, a kitchen, and a dining room. The house also had a staff of human servants who tended to the horse's every need, including brushing his coat, massaging his legs, and singing him lullabies at night. Incitatus even had his own guard to watch over him day and night to make sure he was safe from harm.

It's not really clear why Caligula chose to make Incitatus a senator. Some historians say he did it as a joke to make fun of the Roman Senate, which he supposedly despised. Others believe he did it to show off his power and prove he could accomplish whatever he desired, even if it was ridiculous. Point proven.

Whatever his intentions, Caligula treated the situation seriously. He dressed Incitatus in a senatorial toga and had him participate in political meetings with other senators. The rest of the Senate must have felt pretty awkward sitting at a table with a robed horse. Also, Caligula commanded that Incitatus be called "Lord Incitatus" and that the Senate's official records be updated to reflect Incitatus' views on important issues. The horse probably disagreed with everyone since all he could say was "Nay."

But a disagreeable horse didn't stop Caligula from planning to make Incitatus a consul, one of the highest positions in the Roman government. A consul was like a president or a prime minister, someone with enormous power and influence. It was a position reserved for the most talented and experienced politicians. Fortunately, or unfortunately, depending on your point of view, Caligula's plans were never realized. In 41 AD, he was assassinated by a group of conspirators who had grown tired of his erratic behavior and tyrannical rule. People could only put up with a horse-obsessed ruler for so long. Incitatus, on the other hand, lived a long and happy life until he died of natural causes at the ripe old age of eight.

Part 3: The Breakdown

What can we learn from this weird historical event? Well, for one thing, it shows how absolute power can corrupt even the most rational and intelligent people. Although Caligula wasn't as dumb as those folks who believed they were made of glass, his infatuation with his horse and desire to make fun of the Senate led him to act in an odd and grotesque manner. It also shows how dangerous it is to have leaders who are detached from reality and who prioritize their own whims over the needs of their people.

Although the story of Caligula and his horse senator may appear humorous, it contains some significant lessons for us to take away. Let's hope our current leaders don't get any ideas about turning their pets or favorite animals into political appointees. It'd be weird if a zoo opened up at the White House.

CHAPTER 12:
A SPOONFUL OF KETCHUP

Part 1: The Fact

In the mid-1800s, people searched high and low for the perfect quick fix to get rid of that pestering cough or stomachache. Suddenly, a new miracle cure came to town, and it came in the unexpected form of ketchup. Ketchup, believe it or not, was sold as a cure for everything under the sun from jaundice to indigestion to rheumatism. It wasn't just any old ketchup. It was medicinal ketchup made with all sorts of special ingredients. At least it probably would have been a tasty medicine.

Part 2: The Story

This odd ketchup craze started with Dr. John Cook Bennett. Dr. Bennett was a physician and botanist who believed tomatoes had amazing medicinal properties. He wasn't too far off. Tomatoes were never meant to be a source of medicine or a remedy for any sickness, but they are extremely healthy vegetables (technically, they're a fruit since they fit the botanical definition of one, but for culinary purposes, we call them veggies). Tomatoes have important nutrients like vitamin C and potassium. They're rich in antioxidants, can help reduce the risk of heart disease and certain cancers, and can help with our body's healing process. This doctor probably wasn't aware of most of these benefits, especially since the mid-1800s was a time when you found tomatoes in decorative flower pots rather than on plates. It looked like Dr. John Cook Bennett took his name a little too seriously; he should have stayed in his medical field rather than try to "cook."

At first, people questioned this supposed miracle ketchup, but Dr. Bennett was a persuasive guy. Soon enough, people started to believe him and plenty of other doctors and salespeople trying to sell the stuff. Manufacturers started making medicinal ketchup with all sorts of special ingredients, like cayenne pepper and cloves. There were even ketchup pills, little capsules filled with tomato extract.

The newspapers went wild with stories of miraculous cures. One ad claimed that a man who had broken his leg was completely cured after taking medicinal ketchup for just one week. Not even medicine designed to cure broken bones can cure broken bones in just one week. Another story said that a woman who had been bedridden with rheumatism for several years was able to walk again after taking tomato pills. She probably just took many pills and needed to run to the bathroom.

As time passed, people started to realize these claims were too good to be true. They tried the ketchup and the pills but didn't see any results. Soon enough, the public lost faith in medicinal ketchup. By 1850, the craze was over, and people had moved on to other cures.

Part 3: The Breakdown

It's easy to chuckle now that the ketchup craze has passed since it all seems so absurd. But it also serves as a reminder of how impressionable we are to hype and unrealized promises. With his magnetic personality, Dr. Bennett persuaded patients that something as commonplace as ketchup could treat their ailments. And for a time, people believed him.

Similar patterns can be seen in the health and wellness industry today. There are several medicines and therapies that promise to be miracle treatments for everything from cancer to weight loss. And while some of these treatments are authentic, it's important to approach them with a critical eye. Especially when it comes to our health, we can't always believe everything we read or hear.

Let's not forget about ketchup's ultimate purpose as a condiment while we're on the subject. The popularity of ketchup, in that sense, may have taken a few more years to catch on, but once it did, there was no turning back. Today, ketchup is a staple in households around the world, and we can't imagine our burgers and fries without it.

Part 4: The Sketch

Dr. Bennett squinted through his spectacles at a bottle containing a thick, dark liquid. Its density made it almost impossible to see the flickering candlelight behind it.

After giving the bottle a quick swirl, he nodded in satisfaction and sealed the bottle with a flat cap. Placing it beside a pyramid of similar bottles, he gazed proudly at an advertisement poster hanging on the wall. Despite his lack of artistic talent, he believed the poster conveyed the essence of a desperately ill child wishing to play and engage in other activities they were too sick to do. He felt confident "Dr. Bennett's Miracle Ketchup" would sell like hotcakes. In fact, his modest practice had grown considerably in the recent weeks following the launch of his miraculous concoction.

"Dr. Bennett!"

The doctor looked up from his desk and saw his assistant, Wendell, rush through the door. The college boy had to quickly halt on his heels before colliding with the desk and disrupting the ketchup pyramid.

"Not so fast, Wendell!" Dr. Bennett hollered, bracing himself to catch any bottles in case they fell. "Don't worry. Pretty soon, I'll be able to afford a much larger office that's not in the back of this pharmacy. This place is so small that my legs are all bruised from testing people's reflexes."

Wendell smiled weakly and held out a bag. "I got the tomato plant like you wanted. This one shouldn't shrivel up as fast. We can make a lot more ketchup now-"

Dr. Bennett waved his hands in alarm. "Wendell, close the door!"

"Right." Wendell shut the door and turned back to the doctor. "Sorry."

Dr. Bennett sighed with relief and snatched the bag. "I don't want anyone seeing us squeezing our own tomatoes. Making my miracle ketchup is supposed to be much more complicated than that." He hid the bag in a drawer with his physician's kit containing a stethoscope, glass thermometer, fiddle strings for stitching, and bullet probes. "Wendell, is my first patient for the day here yet?"

Wendell's eyes widened. "Oh! Yes! I forgot about her."

"Can you bring her in?"

"Do you want me to carry her…?"

Dr. Bennett thrust the door open and pushed Wendell out. "Just tell her to come in. It's not rocket science. It can't be since there's no such thing as rocket science yet. Why, hello there!" He flashed a huge smile at a middle-aged woman with a springy bell-shaped skirt as she walked into his office. He shut the door behind her and asked, "What can I do for you?"

"My name is something from the 1800s," the woman blurted out. "Beulah, to be more specific."

"What seems to ail you?" Dr. Bennett asked.

Beulah shrugged. "I suffer from hypertension, but no one knows because it's not a word yet."

"Do you have a physical ailment?" Dr. Bennett asked, ignoring her comment.

Beulah fidgeted with her skirt. "Well, a centipede is coming out of my body."

Dr. Bennett's eyebrows shot up like two rockets that weren't invented yet. "Are you referring to a tapeworm?"

"I don't know. Are tapeworms worms that like to tape things?"

"They're like tapeworms."

"That doesn't answer my question."

"Well, lucky for you," Dr. Bennett said cheerfully while snapping his fingers, "I have the perfect cure for you." He slid behind his desk and held up one of his precious ketchup bottles in a stance as if he was on one of his posters. "This is my new miracle medicine. Ketchup!"

Beulah grunted. She didn't seem too impressed. "What does catching up have to do with anything?"

"It's ketchup," Dr. Bennett tried to explain. "It's a tomato-based medicine. Tomato has several miraculous healing properties. I was one of the first to discover that, if I do say so myself."

"You did say so yourself since you were the only one talking," Beulah said. She snatched the bottle and sniffed it. "I don't smell anything. Oh, I haven't opened it yet." She looked up at Dr. Bennett with pleading eyes. "Dr. Bennett! I'm having a difficult time. I need a cure-all!"

"I'm giving it to you!" Dr. Bennett yelled, pointing at the bottle in her hand.

Beulah blinked in a daze. "Oh. Well, obviously I have issues. At least I don't think I'm made of glass because that'd be dumb."

"Well, this ketchup will cure you and everything that ails you," Dr. Bennett said proudly, patting the top bottle in his pyramid. "Just look at the poster." He pointed to his picture of the depressed child with a thermometer hanging out his mouth. "As the poster says, it's ketchup with life!"

Beulah looked askance at the poster. "Wow. That kid looks not happy."

"Imagine that's you," Dr. Bennett told her, "because you're also not happy and wish to be happy without your ailments. My ketchup will fulfill your wish to become happy again without your ailments."

"I believe every word you're saying right now," Beulah said blankly.

"Take a bottle of ketchup, and be cured!" Dr. Bennett thundered.

"I'll be cured!" Beulah shouted, raising her bottle into the air. "Oh, the salvation in this bottle! Cure me! Cure me, I say!"

Dr. Bennett held out his hand. "That'll be $200."

Beulah's smile vanished instantly. "Say what?"

"The bottle is $200," Dr. Bennett told her casually, "which may be around $6,000 in the 21st century, so you're definitely getting a good bargain today by purchasing it now."

"I do love a good bargain," Beulah said. "I will send the money by horseback."

"Wonderful," Dr. Bennett said, flashing his smile again. "Good day, Beulah."

"It better be."

Dr. Bennett opened the door for Beulah and watched her walk back out into the pharmacy. He saw her open the cap and sniff the contents. She disappeared behind a row of molasses cans, but he was pretty sure she had just started guzzling the entire bottle.

"Dr. Bennett?" Wendell chirped, popping out of nowhere. "Your next patient is ready."

"Wonderful," Dr. Bennett said happily. "I just made $200, Wendell. I can buy myself a whole year's supply of dried apples. Why, hello!" He smiled again as two men stepped into his office.

"My name is Clarence," the first man said, tipping his hat. Motioning to the other man, he said, "This is Eugene, my *friend*." He emphasized this last word with air quotes.

Eugene nearly gagged on his overly large handlebar mustache. "Whoa. Hold up there. What were those air quotes for?"

Clarence shrugged. "Because you're really my brother."

"Then why didn't you just say that?"

Clarence shrugged again. "I don't know. I guess I'm demented. That's why I'm here, Doctor. I need some kind of medicine to help me stop being so demented."

It took a moment for Dr. Bennett to realize the man was serious. "Oh. Well, do I have the perfect cure for you."

"There's more," Eugene added. "We both have the flu. And brain troubles."

"Oh, perfect!" Dr. Bennett cooed.

"Perfect?" Eugene snapped. "You're calling our suffering perfect?"

"I meant *you're* perfect," Dr. Bennett quickly said.

"Oh, thanks!"

"Anyway…" Dr. Bennett took a bottle off the top row of his pyramid. "My ketchup is a perfect relief and cure for the flu, the cold, brain damage, headaches, fatigue, sleeplessness, hangovers, coughs, throat troubles, shaking hands, wobbly legs, balding, broken bones, seasickness, cold sweats, indigestion, and flatulence."

Clarence perked up. "Well, great! We're suffering from all of that too. Except flatulence."

"Ketchup can cure all that?" Eugene asked slowly.

Dr. Bennett sensed the skepticism in his voice. "It's the miracle of ketchup."

"Oh, okay."

Clarence laughed. "I had no idea something so simple as squeezed tomato could be so effective. I should just make my own ketchup-"

"No!" Dr. Bennett shouted, maybe a little too forcefully. He quickly brought himself back down a notch and smiled. "No, the average person cannot make medicinal ketchup. Only doctors can make it."

"With love?" Eugene asked.

"Yes."

"Wow, he said yes."

"A bottle is only $300," Dr. Bennett said.

"Really?" Eugene spluttered. "I can buy a whole year's supply of white sugar for that much." He picked up a bottle and weighed it thoughtfully in his hand. "Well, I guess this one bottle of ketchup is more important than a whole year's supply of sugar. I mean, $300 does sound like a reasonable amount for pulverized tomato innards."

"Let's buy it," Clarence said excitedly. "I believe every word Dr. Bennett has said. I mean, a squeezable cure for every single sickness on the planet made from tomatoes is totally believable. Thanks, Doc!"

"We'll send the money by horse," Eugene said.

"I'll be expecting it," Dr. Bennett said, opening the door. "Have a wonderful day! Don't forget to come back for another bottle when you're finished!" Dr. Bennett stopped waving as soon as the two men disappeared. "I thought they'd never leave. They do too suffer from flatulence."

Wendell popped in out of nowhere again. "Dr. Bennett, somebody spilled ketchup out here."

"What?"

Dr. Bennett nearly jumped as Beulah came shuffling back into his office.

"Excuse me, Doctor."

Dr. Bennett eyed the mess of ketchup all over Beulah's face. "Do you need some more ketchup?"

Beulah licked her lips. "I believe I do."

"What happened to your first bottle?"

Beulah wiped her hands on her skirt. "Well, you see, I walked outside into the New York City streets when somebody was like, 'I have an invention for a lightbulb!' And I was like, 'That's dumb!' So I took it from him and threw it in the street, and it shattered. So then I was like, 'I sure hope that didn't affect history.' And oh yeah, I dropped my ketchup in the process."

"Well, here's another bottle," Dr. Bennett said, handing her another. "That's $250."

"Didn't I pay $200 last time?" Beulah asked suspiciously.

"No."

Beulah stared at the doctor for a moment. "Well, then fine. I'll send you the money via horse." She grabbed the bottle and lovingly wrapped her arms around it. "I'm so glad this isn't a ripoff." She waved her fingers in farewell at Dr. Bennett and scurried back out into the pharmacy.

"Are there any more patients?" Dr. Bennett called out.

"Not right now," Wendell said. "There is a problem, though."

"What is it?"

Wendell pointed into the pharmacy. "The pharmacist is selling tomato plants… as indoor decor."

Dr. Bennett eyes nearly popped out of his skull. Grinding his teeth, he said, "We can't have that. We must make the public realize tomatoes are for medicine and not dining table centerpieces!" He hurtled past Wendell and found the pharmacist dusting off his tomato plants he had just set by the front window. "You there! Pharmacist!"

The older man looked up. "My name's Lester."

"Like it matters."

"It does if you're trying to address me."

"Oh. True." Dr. Bennett pointed to the tomato plants. "Lester, what is the meaning of this?"

"I'm not a dictionary."

"And tomato plants aren't for decoration," Dr. Bennett snapped. "Don't you realize tomatoes have the powerful power of medical practices?"

Lester didn't seem too convinced. "They do?"

Dr. Bennett plucked a tomato from one of the plants and gently squeezed it in his hand. "Within these spherical red hallow walls is the answer to any sickness or ailment you may have."

"I do have wobbly legs," Lester said.

"What a coincidence," Dr. Bennett said in amazement. "Wobbly legs is on the list of things that ketchup cures!"

"Really?" Lester cried, taking the tomato. "If ketchup is inside the tomato, I should just eat tomatoes then." Before he could take a bite, Dr. Bennett snatched the tomato away. "That's not how it works. Medicinal ketchup can only be prescribed by a doctor."

"But you just said the ketchup is inside the tomato."

"It is."

"So why can't I just eat the tomato and be cured?"

"Because the ketchup inside this particular tomato isn't from a doctor."

Lester narrowed his eyes in thought. "I feel like there's something not right somewhere."

"You're right!" Dr. Bennett said. "What's not right are your wobbly legs. Luckily for you, I have several bottles of ketchup you can buy from my personal stock right here and right now for only $350."

Lester shook his head. "No."

Dr. Bennett froze. "No?"

Lester stood his ground. "No." He picked up one of the tomato plants. "I just so happen to have a medical license, which makes me a doctor. Therefore, any ketchup I make will be medicinal. I think I'll take it one step further and sell tomato pills. The public would love that. I'm going to be rich. I'll finally be able to afford my own patch of land in the Atlantic Ocean. Thanks for the tip, Doc." Lester scooped up another plant and hobbled out of sight.

With a nervous twitch in his cheek, Dr. Bennett tossed the tomato he had been holding over his shoulder. He bolted past Wendell, failing to notice the tomato dripping down his assistant's frowning face.

CHAPTER 13:
HAVING A SWELL TIME

Part 1: The Fact

It was an exciting day in 1966 when scientists tested the latest and greatest spacesuit. The air buzzed with anticipation and excitement. Humanity had at last developed a way to escape the limits of our planet and travel into the vastness of space. But as with most things involving cutting-edge technology, things didn't go as planned. The man inside the suit was exposed to a total vacuum for 30 seconds.

Part 2: The Story

Jim LeBlanc was a brave man who volunteered to wear what was called a moon suit prototype. As he stepped into the vacuum chamber wearing the moon suit, his heart surely raced with anticipation. No human had ever been exposed to the vacuum of space before. The vacuum in the front closet was as far as anyone had gotten. The crew believed everything would proceed without a hitch, but they couldn't have been more wrong. That sounded so ominous.

Jim felt pressure growing in his ears as soon as the vacuum was induced inside the chamber. This meant there was no air or atmospheric pressure. The rising pressure in his ears should have been the only warning sign he needed to call the test off. The moon suit clearly wasn't doing its job. What he didn't know was that the hose that supplied the air to his suit had become detached. Nothing he did could release the pressure in his ears. He tried yawning and swallowing, but that didn't help. Soon, he started to feel like his eardrums were about to burst.

While the pressure in his ears continued building, something else started to happen. Jim began experiencing a tingling sensation. It was as though each cell in his body was being torn apart. His lungs felt like they were collapsing, and he could feel his blood boiling. He knew he was in serious trouble. The staff outside the chamber was equally in panic mode but probably not as much since they weren't about to be pulled apart by an invisible force. They had never seen anything like this before, and they didn't know what to do. But they couldn't just stand there and watch Jim slowly die in front of them. They had to act fast.

One of the scientists sprinted over to the control panel and began frantically pressing buttons. The rest of the staff scrambled to understand what was happening and devise a plan to save Jim. After what felt like an eternity, which in reality was a quick 25 seconds, the scientists finally stopped the vacuum. Jim was taken to the hospital, where he ended up fully recovering. The doctors found it hard to believe. Even though it was supposed to be impossible, Jim had managed to survive being exposed to a complete vacuum. He only left with an earache.

LeBlanc later recalled, "As I stumbled backward, I could feel the saliva on my tongue starting to bubble just before I went unconscious, and that's the last thing I remember." Imagine you find yourself in the vacuum of space, which should hopefully be a very unlikely scenario. In that case, the first thing to happen is asphyxiation, or the lack of oxygen, in the bloodstream. You'll lose consciousness after about 15 seconds, and your body will start to swell due to the loss of atmospheric pressure after about 30. That's probably where the tongue bubbling comes in. Any air left in your lungs will cause them to rupture, and any oxygen in the rest of your body will start making your body swell twice its normal size. The skin is elastic enough to keep the body from exploding, though. Death occurs at around 90 seconds.

Part 3: The Breakdown

This spacesuit test was an important turning point in the history of space exploration. It demonstrated mistakes could still be made despite careful planning and preparation. It serves as a clear reminder that the universe is a harsh, unforgiving place that calls for cautious and careful planning. Despite all of our modern developments, nature still has the final say.

The incident taught us to be modest and respectful of nature's forces if anything else. Nothing should be taken for granted, and we should always be ready for the worst. We also need to be open to learning from our mistakes and have a healthy respect for the unknown. Only then can we hope to achieve great things and progress toward a better future. Being careless and exploding won't get us anywhere, after all.

CHAPTER 14:
FAKE PARIS

Part 1: The Fact

When you paint a picture of Paris in your mind, you might think of the Eiffel Tower, the Louvre, or a delicious croissant. You'll find all of this in the fake Paris, too. Well, maybe not the croissant since no one actually lived in this fake Paris.

During World War II, the French built a true-to-life replica of the city- a counterfeit, phony, fictitious imitation of Paris. It wasn't because they needed to double the size of the city to hold all the tourists. It was an attempt to protect the real Paris from German bombers and fighters during the war.

Part 2: The Story

The Germans had created the zeppelin by 1917, a new weapon they could use to attack cities from the sky. These enormous airships were nearly impossible to shoot down and could carry tons of bombs. The French military came up with a strategy to defend Paris that involved creating an exact copy of the city to confuse the Germans. If there was a list called "How to Protect Paris" with 100 ideas on it, you'd think building an exact copy of the city would be at the bottom since that wasn't something you could exactly do overnight. Kudos to the French for thinking outside the box. They built a mock version of Paris complete with imitations of well-known sites, including the Champs-Elysées, the Gard du Nord train station, and the River Seine.

The fake Paris was built in a region called Seine-et-Marne, 15 miles from the actual Paris. Its strategic location made it difficult for German planes to find because it was close to a forest and other natural barriers. The French constructed the fictional city from plaster, canvas, and wood. They even went so far as to replicate nighttime street lamps by using fake lights.

The fake city was so expertly planned that it resembled the actual Paris almost exactly. The buildings were built with the same height and shape as the real ones, and the streets were the same width. The French, however, hoped that a few minor changes would deceive the German pilots. For instance, the original Eiffel Tower is nearly 300 meters tall, whereas the copy was barely 60 meters. The idea was to make the fake city seem less significant and smaller than the real one.

The French didn't just build a fake city to trick the German forces, though. They also made sure the real Paris was dark during the night by implementing a strict blackout policy. At night, the city's lights were all turned off, and residents were told to cover their windows with dark curtains. Because of this, German pilots frequently confused the phony city with the real city and found it difficult to distinguish between the two.

The fake Paris was only used for a short while since the war ended soon after its construction. The city was then deserted and left in ruins. However, the French military used many of the buildings for target practice, so today, very little of the fake city remains. That was probably for the best because if a tourist stumbled upon it today, they'd probably think Paris had been evacuated and ransacked due to a zombie apocalypse.

Part 3: The Breakdown

The French weren't the only ones who built replica cities during World War II. To trick the Germans, the British built a fake village called "Dunham-on-Trent." It was built to look like a weapons factory down to the phony buildings, storage tanks, and railways.

The creation of the fake Paris may seem a little over the top, but it was a pretty clever strategy to keep the real city from danger. It demonstrated how ingenious and inventive people can be in the midst of a battle. The creation of the fake Paris was a monument to the effectiveness of deceit in some ways. Similar strategies are being used by numerous nations today to safeguard their national security. For instance, nations may build fake military installations to fool their adversaries or use false information to mislead them.

The building of the fake Paris also teaches us the importance of creativity and innovation during times of crisis. It's easy to become careless when faced with challenges, but history has shown us that the most successful strategies are often the most creative and weird ones.

CHAPTER 15:
EDISON'S CREEPY DOLL

Part 1: The Fact

Thomas Edison was a brilliant inventor who gave us many amazing things that we can't imagine living without like the lightbulb, the movie camera, and the photograph. Of his 1,093 patents, one stands out as particularly odd and creepy. That would be his invention of the talking doll. In 1890, Edison created a line of baby dolls called Edison's Phonograph Dolls. They were one of his rare inventions that didn't quite take off as expected. The reason is the stuff of nightmares, as they were just too creepy.

Part 2: The Story

The dolls looked innocent enough. They had wooden bodies and porcelain heads, and they had tiny phonographs in their chests that could play recordings of nursery rhymes like "Hickory Dickory Dock," "Now I Lay Me Down to Sleep," and "Twinkle Twinkle Little Star." On the surface, the idea of the talking dolls sounded impressive, and kids were excited to get their hands on them. However, the dolls only stayed in production for six weeks. So what went wrong?

It turned out the dolls were just plain too creepy for kids to handle. You'd agree if you heard a recording of one of these dolls. Just search for Edison's dolls online, and you'll find videos of what these dolls sounded like. Some of the shrill and garbled recordings sound like distorted voices wailing and shouting from an underwater grave. Hearing a high-pitched voice shouting at you like it's putting a curse on you while you're trying to sleep in a dark room is pretty disturbing. If you get the chance to listen to one of these dolls, prepare your spine because the chills will come knocking. These sounds were definitely not the sweet and soothing lullabies children were used to.

Apart from the creepy recordings, the dolls also had other problems. They broke easily, the sound quality didn't last very long, and the mini phonographs kept breaking. Not to mention, they cost way too much, something like almost $300 in today's money. That was a lot of money back in 1890, especially for a doll that didn't work properly and popped out of a horror movie filmed on one of Edison's movie cameras.

Part 3: The Breakdown

The Edison Phonograph Dolls were a commercial failure, but they remain an interesting footnote in history. It's interesting to think about the fact that over a century ago, people were trying to combine technology with toys. It was a bold and novel idea, but it just didn't quite work out. Looking back at the history of the Edison Phonograph Dolls, it's clear that not every new invention will succeed. Even someone as brilliant as Thomas Edison had a few misses along the way. It's a reminder that failure is a natural part of the creative process and that even the most brilliant minds can't always predict what will catch on with the public. Thankfully, Edison kept working on the lightbulb instead of giving that up to work on a talking doll.

In today's world, we still see people trying to combine technology with toys, although the results are usually a lot less frightening than the Edison Phonograph Dolls. Virtual reality headsets, smart toys, and interactive games are just a few examples of how technology is being used to enhance the toy experience. However, the Edison Phonograph Dolls serve as a cautionary tale about the risks of putting too much emphasis on technology at the expense of other factors, like the quality of the product and its marketability.

CHAPTER 16:
THE NOVL WITH NO "E"

Part 1: The Fact

Need another book to read after this one? This week's literary pick is *Gadsby* by Ernest Vincent Wright. Don't get it confused with *The Great Gatsby*, the 1925 novel by F. Scott Fitzgerald, especially since *The Great Gatsby* has an E in the title. *Gadsby* was a novel that defied all literary norms when it was published in 1939 because not one of its 50,000 words had the letter E in them. That's impossible. There are 50 E's in this paragraph alone.

Part 2: The Story

The story of *Gatsby* takes place in the fictional town of Branton Hills, which is on the verge of ruins. John Gadsby, the city's youth organizer, attempts to save the neighborhood so all is not lost. Gadsby brings the residents of Branton Hills together using his charm and leadership abilities, and they all start to work on plans for a better future for their beloved town.

Now pay attention to the opening sentence of *Gatsby*: "If youth, throughout all history, had had a champion to stand up for it; to show a doubting world that a child can think; and, possibly, do it practically; you wouldn't constantly run across folks today who claim that 'a child don't know anything.'" Yep, not a single E. Plenty of grammatical mistakes, though. It can be difficult to actually understand what the sentence means.

You're probably wondering why Ernest Vincent Wright decided not to use the letter E when writing his book. Was he trying to write something original, or did he give himself some type of literary challenge? Actually, Wright was trying to make a point. He thought that an over-reliance on some letters held back a writer's creativity, especially with the letter E. Wright intended to show that you could make an engaging story without using the most common letter in the English language.

It's tough to imagine how challenging it is to write a novel without ever using the letter E. Write a random sentence. The letter E will surely pop up more than once in maybe every other word or so that you write. It's really difficult to ignore because it's so ingrained in our vocabulary. It's a wonder how Wright was able to pull it off. He had to use words many people had never heard of to improve his vocabulary. For instance, he wrote, "Call it tornado, volcano, military onslaught, or what you will, this town found that it had a bunch of kids who had wills that would admit of no snoozing; for that is Youth, on its forward march of inquiry, thought and action." In other words, Wright's saying the town had a lot of high-energy kids. Or you can come up with your own meaning.

Despite being a literary oddity, *Gadsby* garnered some favorable reviews when it was first released in 1939. Critics complimented Wright for his originality and his ability to convey a captivating story without the use of the letter E. On the flip side, a large number of people also believed that the book was a terrible waste of time and that there was no point in reading a book that required so much effort to understand.

Part 3: The Breakdown

Gadsby is more than just a literary study. It's a critique of the state of writing and the constraints we place on ourselves as authors. Wright encouraged other writers to think outside the norm and discover fresh methods to innovate.

The novel serves as a reminder that it's okay to occasionally break the rules. We won't ever push ourselves to be truly innovative if we keep doing the same old routines day after day. Try challenging yourself to do something unusual when you're given a writing assignment. Even if you can't write a complete novel without using the letter E, you can still surprise yourself by stepping outside your comfort zone. There are no boundaries to what we can achieve if we let go of our assumptions and just let ourselves have fun.

Fun fact: this entire chapter was written without the letter X. Is anyone impressed?

CHAPTER 17:
JACK THE SIGNALBABOON

Part 1: The Fact

Have you checked lately who or what you're working with? You might want to double check that your coworkers are human and not chacma baboons because chacma baboons have a detailed work history. In 1882, a chacma baboon received 20 cents a day for working as a signalman at a South African train station. Odd picture there. First off, a signalman is someone who uses levers or handles to switch the train signals whenever a train approaches. Secondly, a chacma baboon is a largest monkey that lives primarily in southern Africa. Third off, 20 cents in 1882 is equivalent to almost seven bucks today.

Part 2: The Story

The story of this chacma baboon named Jack is a truly remarkable one. James Edwin Wide was the one who discovered Jack. James, who walked around on two wooden peg legs after losing both his legs as a result of a neurotic habit of jumping between moving railway cars, needed some assistance to carry out his daily activities. That was when he came across Jack in a South African market. The baboon was already known in the area for his unique abilities. He was a large and intelligent chacma baboon trained to perform various tasks, including driving an oxcart around the market. James immediately became drawn to Jack's intelligence and decided to take him under his wing- or tail to be anatomically correct. James and Jack, the dynamic duo!

The first thing James did was train Jack to push him around in a small trolley so that he could move around with ease. The half-mile walk to his job at the train station was understandably too difficult for him. Over time, Jack became an indispensable companion to James, helping him with different household chores like sweeping and taking out the trash. Nevertheless, the bond between the two grew stronger with each passing day.

One day, James had an idea. He wondered if he could train Jack to do his job as a signalman at the local train station. It was a dangerous job requiring quick reflexes and a sharp mind, but James was confident in Jack's abilities and decided to let him try. Going from taking out the trash to controlling trains was a pretty big leap, but it sounded like James had all the confidence in the world in Jack.

It wasn't long before Jack was fully trained and performing the duties of a signalman with ease. He used the levers and handles to switch the train signals whenever a train approached, just like any human signalman would. James was amazed by Jack's ability to learn and perform such a difficult task. He was also proud to have a companion who could share his passion for trains and the railway industry.

Eventually, a train passenger noticed the baboon changing the signals, and they complained to the railway company. Customer service existed even back then, apparently. The railway company sent someone out to test Jack's abilities. They found the baboon completely capable of doing the job so let him continue working. It's said Jack never made one single mistake in his nine years of working as a signalman.

Part 3: The Breakdown

Jack's story demonstrates our views toward both labor and animals. The fact that a baboon could carry out the responsibilities of a signalman demonstrates the extraordinary intelligence and adaptability of creatures like Jack.

Issues like worker rights and animal welfare are still heated topics today. Even though we've made progress in stopping animal exploitation and cruelty, there's still a lot to be done to make sure animals are treated with respect and dignity. Although it's unlikely baboons will be operating subway trains anytime soon, Jack's story also demonstrates how animals have the potential to make significant contributions to humanity. It's just important that we treat these animals kindly while exploring their capabilities.

This piece of weird history tells us we should respect the potential and intelligence of every living thing, regardless of species. It also emphasizes the need for us to consider the moral ramifications of our actions and how we interact with animals more carefully. James and Jack remind us of our responsibility to protect the environment and the importance of showing love and respect to all living things.

Part 4: The Sketch

A sweltering sun flared down through a gap in the clouds onto the roof of a small shack slightly elevated on a wooden platform. In the cramped interior, James sat on a wobbly stool beside the open door, hoping to catch the faint whiff of a cool breeze. His companion was trying to do the same and probably had more luck since he was sitting on the roof.

"Jack!" James grabbed a broom and jabbed the wooden ceiling. "Are you up there, Jack? You know I can't climb up there with you. Having two pieces of wood for feet doesn't exactly make me an expert climber. I am rather good at tap dancing, though." He began tapping his two peg legs in a rhythmic pattern. That seemed to catch Jack's attention. James ducked as his companion swung through the open door. "Hello, Jack!"

Hoo hoo!

James grinned and patted Jack's head. Jack was the perfect partner out there at the signal station. Jack was a chacma baboon who had coarse gray fur and a long, almost humorous downward-sloping face. His canine teeth were always poking out of his mouth, so Jack always looked like he was smiling. James liked to think the baboon must have really enjoyed being there at the station with him.

James grabbed the broom in both hands and pulled himself up. "Well, Jack? Ready to learn the job and make the trains not crash?"

Jack twisted his head around and looked at James as if saying, "Yes, sir! I'm sure ready!"

"Come along then, Jack!"

James grabbed his signalman's hat and hobbled onto the station platform. He looked both ways down the tracks and saw nothing but the open expanse of scorched grass and wilting trees. He waved the dust out of his face and took his place beside a row of six levers on the edge of the platform. "Now listen, Jack. I'm going to teach you how to change the signals. Changing the signals decides which track the train will go. Do you think you can handle this?"

Hoo hoo!

Jack scratched his head and leaned against one of the levers. The lever jerked forward, startling the baboon enough to make him start howling and jumping up and down.

"It's okay!" James cried, waving his arms. "You actually just did what you were supposed to do. Good job, Jack! Pull the lever again. That's it."

James watched Jack slide over to the second lever. The baboon inspected it for a minute and then stuck his mouth around the end. "That's not a banana, Jack," James said, shaking his head.

Jack yanked back the lever and looked at James as if for approval.

"Perfect!" James exclaimed. "You got this in the bag. No, there is no bag. So Jack, you pull these levers when a train comes. You know, train. Do you know what a train is?"

Hoo hoo!

"I think you meant to say 'choo choo.' Very good!"

"Excuse me, kind fellow."

James spun around and saw a woman in a long dress with long sleeves and plenty of perspiration on her face standing at the other edge of the platform. "Where did you come from, ma'am?"

"What an inappropriate comment," the woman said, whipping out a fan. She started furiously fanning herself, which only made the sweat fly into her eyes more. "I am here for the train. When is the train due?"

James looked around. Where did this woman come from? They were in the middle of nowhere down there in South Africa. The only thing around was this tiny signal station. "Ma'am, you do know this isn't a train station?"

The woman slapped her fan on a sign on the side of the shack that said *Signal Station*. "This is a station, is it not?"

James nervously twisted his handlebar mustache. "Well, yes. This is a station, but not the kind of station where passengers board and exit the train."

"I fail to understand what you're saying," the woman ranted.

"That's not my problem."

"Eek!" The woman abruptly screeched. "What is that clump of fur?" She pointed her fan at Jack, who was busy pulling the levers back and forth.

"That's Jack," James told her. "He works with me."

The woman raised an eyebrow. "A monkey works with you?"

"Quite," James responded proudly.

Pursing her lips, the woman said, "Well, in that case, does he know when the train will arrive? I have an appointment I need to get to in North Africa. That's in the north."

James looked at his pocket watch. "The next train isn't due to pass here for another hour."

"Make it go faster," the woman demanded.

"I can't."

"The service here is atrocious," the woman huffed, turning on her heel. "No one knows when the train is due, the heat is much too much, and there's a monkey monkeying around. I daresay I'm complaining to the railway company."

James watched the woman go, her whiny voice disappearing along with her. *Where is she going?* he wondered. *I hope she's not walking. She's going to get heatstroke in that outfit.*

James looked over at Jack, who was in the process of dragging his behind across the platform. "Hmm. Maybe I should get you a diaper."

"Excuse me, kind fellow."

James spun around again, expecting to see the fanning woman. Instead, he saw a man in a white uniform with a clipboard in hand. "Oh, hello. Now where did you come from?"

The man stepped forward and held out his hand. "My name is Dalton. Sam Dalton. I'm an inspector with the railway company." He noticed James swaying a bit, and his eyes trailed down to James' peg legs. "Uh, what happened here? Our train didn't do that, did it?"

"Oh, it's a long story," James said dismissively, "but I'll tell you anyway. You see, I used to have these sudden urges to climb onto moving trains and jump between the compartments from roof to roof. Needless to say, I no longer have that sudden urge." He kicked up a peg leg for emphasis.

Dalton eyed James in disbelief. "You jumped between compartments on a moving train?"

"Yes."

"Why on earth would you do that?"

James shrugged. "I just did. Isn't that enough?"
"No."

Hoo hoo!

Dalton jumped in fright as Jack ran around James and alighted at his feet. "Uh, what is this?"

"This is Jack," James said. "He's on the payroll."

"He is?" Dalton looked at his clipboard. "Oh. I see. *Jack B. A. Boon - 20 cents per day.* Wow, he's making a lot."

"I know," James said. "I only make 12 cents a day."

"Where did he come from?" Dalton asked.

"I met him at the market," James recounted. "I hired him to push me around in a wheelbarrow since walking around on these peg legs isn't too comfortable for some reason. He did such a great job pushing me around that I decided to teach him how to become a signalman. The two jobs are so relatable."

"Uh huh, sure," Dalton said, nervously fiddling with his clipboard as Jack kept staring at him with his tiny brown eyes behind a bulbous forehead. "Well, that explains my other reasoning for being here. We down at headquarters have been getting some complaints about a baboon working here. They're kind of confused as to why a monkey is screeching at them when they pass by here."

"They have no reason to be frightened," James said.

"I never said they were."

"Everything is fine," James said, patting Jack's shoulder. "He knows what he's doing. He hasn't crashed one single train yet. Then again, no trains have passed by yet."

"Excuse me, kind fellow."

James peered behind Dalton's shoulder and saw a young woman with a pale green parasol in one hand. "Oh, hello. The train doesn't stop here-"

The girl briskly pushed Dalton aside and hurried over to James, where she stuck her parasol under his nose. "The train might not stop here, but animal savagery certainly will!"

"What are you talking about?" James gasped. He stayed as still as possible for fear of the sharp tip of the parasol puncturing his throat. "There's no such thing happening here."

"Is there a chacma baboon in this vicinity?" the girl asked. She looked down and saw the baboon standing beside her. "Apparently, there is. I have visual proof." She moved the parasol downward and stabbed it into James' chest. "My name, for your information, is Bertha, and I'm the co-chair president of the S.P.S.C.B.W.S.S."

"What's that?" James dared to ask.

Bertha narrowed her eyes. "The Society For the Protection Specifically of the Chacma Baboon Working at

Signal Stations. How have you never heard of us? We have a very specific niche, and you literally fit the description to a tee. Speaking of, I would love some tea right now. Do you have any tea?"

"Just nuts," James said, "but that's Jack's lunch. He gets cranky if he doesn't eat."

Bertha rounded on Jack. "Which brings me to the reason why I am here in this desolate area of this one acre of land. Is this baboon being paid well?"

"Twenty cents a day," Dalton informed her.

"Decent," Bertha mused. "Decent. What is he doing with his earnings?"

James shrugged. "I don't know. I'm not his banker."

Bertha bent over to speak to Jack. "I suggest investing in a nice habitat in the Kalahari Desert, dear sir. I hear there are a lot of springboks living there. They make wonderful neighbors."

"Is that all, Bertha?" James asked, wiping his forehead. "Jack needs to get back to work. A train is due here in 20 minutes. It'll be his first train. Hopefully he doesn't overexcite himself and jump in front of it."

"I have another question," Bertha said. "Does Jack have benefits? Like monkey benefits?"

"What are monkey benefits?" Dalton asked.

"Like being able to swing on things if so desired."

"There are trees around here," James pointed out.

"Does Jack have a working bathroom?" Bertha asked.

James pointed behind him. "That ditch over there is good enough."

"Ew!" Bertha cried.

"That's what I use."

"Double ew!" Bertha nearly gagged. "Is there seriously no plumbing yet? What is this, the 19th century? Oomph!" She fully gagged as Jack stuck his fist in her mouth.

"Jack, no!" James shouted. "I know, she's being annoying, but still. It's not polite sticking your hand down someone's throat!" He yanked Jack's hand out of Bertha's mouth and smiled apologetically. "I'm sorry. He's new on the job. He's probably just nervous about signaling his first train. I know I was nervous on my first day. I passed out and fell right on the tracks as a train approached. Now that would have been a much more sensible way to have lost my legs."

Bertha spat out a clump of hair and scratched at her mouth. "That was so disgusting."

"Is Jack okay to keep working, Dalton?" James asked.

"It's fine by me," Dalton replied. "I see no reason why Jack can't perform his duties. What do you think, Bertha?"

Bertha spit out the last remaining baboon hair. "Fine. It's fine. I approve of the baboon working. I want him to have sick days, though. What's he doing now?" Jack had been standing right beside her, pressing his behind into her dress.

Hoo!

"I think he's trying to sit on you," James said.

"Why?"

"I don't know. Maybe he thinks you're a toilet."

Bertha couldn't have looked more offended. "What a thing to say to somebody. Here." She let Jack have her parasol. The baboon yelped in excitement and dashed away with it.

"Well, if that's all," Dalton said, checking his clipboard once again, "I'll be off. We've been getting complaints about another signal station a few miles north. Apparently, there's a giraffe trying to get on the payroll up there. Absurd. So long!"

James waved goodbye and turned his attention to Bertha, who was still spitting out hair. "Are you leaving too?"

Bertha glared at him. "I can take a hint."

"Can you? Can you, though?"

Bertha gathered up her dress and stormed off the platform. "Say goodbye to Jack for me! Remember, the S.P.S.C.B.W.S.S. is watching you!"

James chuckled to himself. There was no need for anyone to watch him and Jack. They were going to do just fine. He looked at his pocket watch again. It was almost time.

"Jack!"

James hobbled back to the levers and peered into the distance. He could see the train as a tiny speck in the distance. "Jack! Your first train!" Jack hopped onto the platform with Bertha's parasol in his mouth. "Forget the parasol, Jack. The lever! You know what to do!"

The train was in sight now. James could see the silhouette of the conductor in the front car. "Now, Jack! Pull the lever! You got this!"

Jack grasped the lever, but instead of pulling it, he used it to steady himself as he tossed the parasol onto the tracks. The train hit the parasol at full speed. Like the sound of a lion attacking a springbok, a terrifying screeching sound filled the air. Metal ground against metal as one of the wheels exploded in an electrifying crack.

James snapped his eyes shut. He didn't want to see it, but he could picture the train derailing and falling onto its side. He slowly opened one eye and peeked down at Jack. The baboon was hopping up and down in giddy excitement. "Uh... okay..." He knew it was too late, but he pulled the lever. "Well, Jack. That was a good practice run." He turned his back to the wreckage. "We'll have you officially begin your new job tomorrow. I just know you'll never make one single mistake as long as you work here!"

CHAPTER 18:
ATTACK OF THE BUNNIES

Part 1: The Fact

It's very therapeutic to picture fluffy, cuddly bunnies hopping over sunny fields and munching on grass and carrots. No stress involved whatsoever. Napoleon Bonaparte probably couldn't do it, though. Picturing cuddly bunnies might have skyrocketed his stress levels. But that's only because a massive horde of escaped rabbits jumping all over him and attacking him might have something to do with it. Not even Napoleon, the most powerful man in Europe in the early 1800s, was a match for a mob of restless rabbits!

Part 2: The Story

In 1807, Bonaparte joined some of his fellow French dignitaries and military officers at a clearing in a forest in the small town of Fontainebleau, where they planned to participate in a traditional rabbit hunt. They were celebrating Bonaparte's recent signing of a couple of peace treaties, one of which, for some reason, took place on a raft in the middle of a river. Little did they know that the rabbits the chief of staff had rounded up for the hunt had a different plan in mind.

As soon as their cages opened, hundreds of rabbits charged straight for Bonaparte and his fellow party companions. Being a rabbit hunt, the rabbits were supposed to run away so the group could hunt them. Instead, the flood of fur was like a scene from a horror movie. The rabbits climbed up the men's legs and even leaped onto Napoleon himself, driven by some mysterious furry agenda.

Imagine being the most powerful person in Europe and coming under attack from a horde of cute bunnies. Talk about embarrassing. The unexpected attack caught Bonaparte off guard. At first, he just laughed it off. Then he realized the rabbits weren't stopping. After they kept jumping all over him, he took off running to try to escape. The rabbits chased after him and actually split into two groups like they were planning to surround him and trap him. Bonaparte couldn't get the rabbits off of him no matter what he did. Eventually, he found a carriage to hide in. The rabbits weren't done with him yet. Some tried to break into the carriage like a group of robbers trying to rob a bank. Not until the carriage rolled away did the rabbits finally stop their attack.

Part 3: The Breakdown

Why did these bunnies decide to rebel against their human counterparts? Was there a secret animal rebellion going on that we were unaware of? This weird piece of history isn't that strange. No, the real reason was much more simple. Napoleon's chief of staff was responsible for getting the rabbits for the hunt, but he made one crucial mistake. He gathered a bunch of domestic rabbits instead of wild rabbits. Wild rabbits would instinctively run away. These domestic rabbits were accustomed to humans. As soon as they were free, they ran toward everyone, thinking they were about to be fed. It wasn't an attack at all. It was just a hectic feeding time at a zoo.

As funny as this whole scenario may have looked, it serves as a reminder for us to respect the environment and the creatures that live in it and be aware of the effects of our actions. It's easy to forget there are so many other species on this earth, and occasionally our actions can have unforeseen effects. If we hope to create a sustainable future for everyone, we must recognize we're not the only residents of this world and must coexist with other species. That doesn't mean walking around with carrots in your pockets in case a rabbit decides to attack, but then again, if a rabbit does attack you when you have a carrot in your pocket, it's because you have a carrot in your pocket. Just don't walk around with carrots in your pocket.

CHAPTER 19:
THE UNDERGROUND MAZE

Part 1: The Fact

Welbeck Abbey never looked the same once John Bentinck, the 5th Duke of Portland, inherited the estate from his father in 1854. Bentinck began a strange and ambitious project on the land, or rather, under it. He transformed 15 miles of tunnels beneath the estate into an underground maze complete with magnificent ballrooms and bedrooms that would have fit smugly in any luxurious castle aboveground. However, no one but the people who dug these rooms ever got the chance to see them.

Part 2: The Story

Bentinck was a bit of an odd guy and had some equally odd habits. He rarely left his bedroom and had his food pushed through a slit in his door. When he did go outside, he wanted people to treat him as if he were a tree and ignore him completely. He always walked around underneath an umbrella and tied his trousers above his ankles with a piece of string. He never wanted to become a Duke. The title was passed onto him after his father died. This was how he inherited the abbey. Instead wishing to focus on his passions for horse racing and the opera, Bentinck now had this massive estate to look after. What do to with it? Dig, of course!

The plan for an elaborate labyrinth seemed reasonable coming from a mind like Bentinck's. The tunnels, which Bentinck and his workers dug themselves, were wide enough for horses and carriages to drive through and even had glass-topped tunnels tall enough for fruit trees to grow. The Duke spent the last 20 years of his reclusive life transforming Welbeck Abbey into one of Europe's most expansive estates.

It isn't very clear why Bentinck built this underground maze. Some say he was trying to keep out of the public eye, while others believe he was just a tad eccentric. Despite his reasons, the Duke's underground labyrinth was certainly impressive. He painted most of the rooms pink, his favorite color. He even built a billiards room, a library, an observatory, and a ballroom that could host 2,000 people. No one ever got the chance to dance in the ballroom, though. Being a recluse, it wasn't exactly a priority of Bentinck's to send out invites to social gatherings.

One of the most fascinating things about the Duke's underground tunnels is that one was so long, it went all the way to the train station in London. Now that was how you avoided traffic. This allowed the Duke to travel to and from London whenever he had to grudgingly appear at the House of Lords without ever having to go outside. He would also disappear into the tunnels through trapdoors without anyone noticing.

Part 3: The Breakdown

Despite the grandeur of the Duke's underground maze, it's a bit of a mystery. For one thing, it's unclear why he spent so much effort creating all of these elaborate rooms that he never really used. It's a shame no one ever used the ballroom. Guests would have loved to experience that, especially since the ceiling was painted to look like the sunset and the only way to get down into it was by an impressive hydraulic lift.

Additionally, the tunnels themselves seemed to have served no practical purpose. The Duke certainly had the means to create something grand and extravagant, but it's not known why he chose to do so underground. The simple truth could be that he just wanted his privacy.

The Duke's project was certainly unusual, but it was also incredibly impressive. Not to mention, his underground maze might serve as a reminder that sometimes the things we come up with aren't always meant to have a practical purpose. Sometimes, we create things simply because we can.

CHAPTER 20:
DIAL THAT CAT

Part 1: The Fact

To all of the cat lovers out there, please know in advance that our feline hero in this story came out just fine in the end after participating in this very weird experiment involving nerves and telephone receivers. This unusual experiment happened in 1929 when the world was still fascinated by the telephone that Alexander Graham Bell had invented more than 50 years before.

For a group of scientists at Princeton University, the telephone that Graham Bell invented just wasn't good enough. Instead of going the obvious route and creating a touchscreen smartphone, they chose to take the invention to the next level by creating the world's first telephone out of a cat.

Part 2: The Story

Again, the cat in this story came out just fine. All it probably had was a headache. The experiment was carried out with the utmost care and precision. Professor Ernst Glen Wever and his research assistant, Charles Bray, were the ones who came up with this crazy idea. Their main goal wasn't to develop a new telephone, though, but to further understand how the auditory nerve perceived sound. The auditory nerve is the nerve that connects the ear to the brain. The common belief before any testing had been done was that if a sound became louder, the pitch of the sound received by the ear should be higher. To prove this, all Wever and Bray needed was a functional nerve to test on. The cat's ears probably perked up when it found out it was going to be the volunteer.

Wever and Bray first put the cat to sleep in order to do the experiment. After it fell asleep, they made a small cut in the cat's skull to reach the auditory nerve. Once they found the nerve, they connected one end of a telephone cable to it. They connected the other end of the cable to a phone receiver. The last completely logical step was to talk into the cat's ears. After Wever stepped into a soundproof room 50 feet away with the receiver in hand, Bray did just that. We don't know exactly what Bray said into the cat's ear, but it was probably something like, "Can you hear me, Wever? I can't believe you're making me communicate with you from inside a sleeping cat's skull." Well, Wever heard him.

The actual experiment involved Bray talking into the cat's ear at different noise levels. When Bray made a sound with a certain frequency into the cat's ear, Wever heard that sound from the receiver at the same frequency. As Bray made another louder sound, Wever heard it, and it was louder. The experiment proved that when a sound got louder, the frequency also increased. That seemed like an obvious deduction, so putting a cat through this traumatic experience was probably not all that necessary.

Part 3: The Breakdown

Despite totally being a tad unconventional, Wever and Bray's research was pioneering. It paved the way for the creation of contemporary hearing aids and cochlear implants. In order to better understand how the brain interpreted sound, they were able to demonstrate that the auditory nerve could convey signals via electrical impulses.

It's interesting to note this wasn't the first time animals had been utilized in research. Animal testing had been a standard practice in research for many years. Animals have been used to increase scientific knowledge and improve human lives in a variety of ways, from researching the effects of radiation on fruit flies to testing cosmetics on rabbits.

This doesn't mean using animals for testing is always right, though. Since many people believe using animals in studies is wrong, there have been many protests about it. While some argue that using animals is required for scientific purposes, others think other, less crude approaches could be taken. Although animal testing has undeniably advanced our understanding of the world, we must always be aware of how our actions affect other living things. We must never lose sight of our humanity as we push science and technology to their limits. Not every cat can survive an upsetting experiment like this one. Actually, the cat didn't survive the second round, but let's not get into that.

CHAPTER 21:
LOVE THAT FIVEHEAD

Part 1: The Fact

Beauty standards are always changing. Some make sense, while others just plain don't. The 1400s was one of these "just plain don't" instances. A lot of really weird beauty trends emerged out of this time period. It was a time when the popular trend was looking as innocent and pure as you could. One of these supposed innocent and pure looks was plucking the eyebrows and hairline to achieve a high, round forehead. Basically, it was a "fivehead," a forehead but with a lot more emphasize on the head.

Part 2: The Story

The fivehead look was popular because hair wasn't fashionable at the time, especially for women. To get that high, round forehead, women plucked away their eyebrows and the hair on their heads. The hairline could go as far back as the top of the scalp. With no hair on the front of the head, women would look like babies, which was the look they were going for. In Renaissance Europe, a high forehead was considered a sign of innocence and purity, and youthfulness was extremely valued. Babies are a sign of pureness and innocence, after all.

Fashion went far beyond hairless faces and high hairlines. When it came to skin, women wanted their skin to look as bright as possible. To achieve a porcelain tone, women ate clay by the handfuls. Clay was believed to purify the body and encourage beautiful skin. Was there proof of this? Ingesting clay would probably do a lot more harm than good. Was risking poisoning and intestinal issues worth it?

Women also applied a lot of white powder in addition to eating clay to get the desired pale complexion. This powder, though, contained white lead, which was poisonous when consumed or absorbed into the skin, along with talc and powdered bone. The powder was mixed with wax, vegetable oil, and whale fat to make it stick to the skin. This resulted in a greasy concoction that wasn't only painful but harmful.

To check off another fashion to-do of the 1400s, fashion-forward women used leeches to make their veins more prominent. They outlined the veins on their chests to make them stand out more. This technique was so common that it helped create the term "blue-blooded." Visible veins were thought to be a sign of good health.

Another weird beauty trend was wiping crocodile feces on the skin. It was believed that crocodile dung could rejuvenate the skin and treat acne, scars, and blemishes. Again, was there proof of this? Did the average person in the 1400s have access to fresh crocodile dung? There's no scientific data that supports these claims, and it's highly suggested to avoid using crocodile dung as a cosmetic treatment- or for anything.

The last beauty tip from the 1400s was squeezing orange juice into the eyes. This was supposed to reduce redness and create clear, bright eyes. First of all, orange juice is acidic. Pouring citric acid into your eyes sounds like it would be something that would *cause* redness unless they didn't think that since oranges were orange and not red. It looked like someone took a page out of Dr. Bennett's book and persuaded people to invest in a cure created from the tomato's distant cousin.

Part 3: The Breakdown

These fashions and beauty standards now look ridiculous to us and even dangerous. They do, however, represent their period's social and cultural norms. People in the 1400s valued youth and purity, and anything that did not conform to this standard was unattractive. While we're not splashing crocodile dung on our faces or plucking our foreheads, there are still some beauty practices out there today that could be somewhat questionable and possibly dangerous. For example, tanning beds and skin bleaching products can possibly result in severe health complications, and the pressure to conform to unrealistic beauty standards can lead to low self-esteem and body image issues.

While the 1400s' views of beauty may seem strange and absurd to us now, they reflect the ideals and viewpoints of the period. It's important to keep in mind there is no universally accepted definition of beauty and that it's a completely subjective concept. We should instead value our individuality and cherish our differences. We should be aware of those beauty trends and behaviors that could be bad for us while also learning from history and appreciating our accomplishments. In the end, being beautiful is more about feeling secure and at ease in our own skin.

Part 4: The Sketch

A line of women stood on a winding stone road, eagerly waiting for their chance to get into the new beauty boutique, the first of its kind in the medieval town. A lavish castle stared down at them from a distant hill as if threatening to banish anyone who didn't look as regal. Excited chatter filled the air as one by one, each woman entered the boutique and came back out with new smiles just as lavish after having the most exclusive beauty treatments performed on them.

Sabina was next. She had flowing, satin-smooth black hair that fell down to her eyes and sun-kissed skin that glowed like a flame. It was horrible. She hated the way she looked. Determined to rid herself of her smooth hair and tanned skin, she waited anxiously in line to get the makeover she'd been dreaming of. As the last customer exited with something orange dripping down her cheeks, Sabina nervously brushed past the giant urn that read "Brenna's Beauty Bash" and maneuvered through some curtains into the boutique.

"About time!" a shrill voice called out. "It's 3:00! Where's my 3:00 appointment?"

"I'm here!" Sabina gasped, clapping giddily.

Out from a beaded curtain came the beautician, Brenna. She oozed beauty. She was the ideal image with a massive, protruding forehead and skin so bright you had to shield your eyes from it. Every woman in the village wanted to look like her. If the term existed in the 1400s, she'd totally be a beauty influencer.

"You're late," Brenna snapped, pointing to a chair. "Somebody didn't check their sundial, did they?"

"I don't have a sundial," Sabina said, taking a seat. "You know how I knew it was 3:00? I knew because three birds flew over my hut."

"That was convenient," Brenna said. With a flick of her wrist, she threw a sheepskin blanket over Sabina's front. "Comfortable?"

"Not really," Sabina said, wrinkling her nose from the stench of the blanket.

"Wonderful."

"I'm Sabina," Sabina said as Brenna spun her chair around to face a mirror bordered with fresh roses.

Sabina grunted. "Did I ask? No. But hello, Sabina. I'm Brenna, as in Brenna. It means either 'little raven' or 'sword,' so you can take your pick."

Sabina frowned. "I think I'll go with 'little raven.' Much more pleasant."

"What does Sabina mean?" Brenna asked while dipping her hands into an urn to clean them.

"Sabina is actually a type of musical instrument," Sabina explained. "It also means 'understanding,' which is ironic because I don't understand much. I mean, like, is the world flat or round? I just don't understand."

Brenna spun around and eyed Sabina. It looked like it took all of her power not to cringe at the sight of her flowing hair and glowing skin. "I see you don't understand anything about beauty."

Sabina shrugged. "I thought my hair looked nice. It's long, silky smooth, even on both sides-"

Brenna vigorously shook her head. "No no no. What is wrong with your, like, face?"

"What do you mean?" Sabina asked. "Did it fall off or something?"

Brenna held up a piece of hay and jabbed it at Sabina's forehead. "What's this stuff all over your forehead?"

Sabina's eyes shot upward. "My eyebrows?"

"No, over your forehead here." Brenna jabbed the hay into Sabina's forehead again.

"My hair?" Sabina guessed.

Brenna nodded. "Yeah. That hair. What is that?"

Sabina's eyes lit up. "Oh! You mean my bangs!"

"Bangs!" Brenna screeched, dropping the hay. "Bangs! Girl, that's so out. No one has bangs. You're basically screaming, 'Look at me! I'm repulsive!' Girl, you have to get rid of those. We have to see that forehead, girl. Actually..." Brenna grabbed Sabina's bangs in one handful and lifted them up like she was opening a cabinet. She tapped Sabina's forehead with a pointy fingernail. "I don't just want to see your forehead. I want to see that fivehead."

"Excuse me?" Sabina said through gritted teeth. She felt like Brenna was trying to pull her bangs out of her skull.

"Your fivehead." Brenna sighed like she was sick and tired of explaining what it meant. "It's like a forehead but more skin." She let go of Sabina's bangs to Sabina's relief and placed a finger on top of Sabina's skull. "This is where your hairline needs to be in order to have that fivehead look. Understand?"

"Well, my name does mean 'understanding,'" Sabina said, "so I guess so. Don't you think that's a little too much forehead?"

Brenna's mouth fell open in complete astonishment. "Seriously? Are you seriously asking me that right now, girl? Look at me!" Brenna tipped her head forward. "Look at my head!" Brenna's hairline arched directly across the top of her skull. Basically, the back half of her head had hair, while the front half was completely bald. "I am beauteous to the max because of this amazing hairstyle. Tell me you don't want to look like this?"

Sabina stared at the hairline. "I just think it looks weird."

"It doesn't," Brenna growled, her bald scalp making her look like a scowling newborn. "I was going to move my hairline all the way back to the base of my scalp and have my hair dangle in the back, but then I realized it'd look like the back of my head had a beard."

"Thanks for that mental image," Sabina said unsurely. "So, I guess you're right about pushing my hairline back. So can you, like, buzz it?"

Brenna waved her hand dismissively. "Of course not."

"Then how can I get my hairline pushed back?" Sabina asked.

Brenna held up a flaming torch. "I can burn it off."

"Hold up!" Sabina shouted, struggling beneath the weight of the heavy sheepskin. "I'm not so sure about that! Wouldn't burning be painful?"

"Just don't touch the fire," Brenna said.

"But wouldn't the fire be on my face?"

"Just your scalp," Brenna said assuredly. "Actually, we can singe those eyebrows off too. I'm actually really surprised you have them. Those are easy to pluck out yourself. You'd look great with no eyebrows, just like me!" Brenna held her torch up to show off her missing eyebrows. The flickering flame made her look like a haunted unpainted doll. "Speaking of your face, have you been eating clay?"

Sabina raised her eyebrows (while she still had them). "Have I been eating clay?"

Brenna moaned. "I take that as a no. I guess it should be obvious with that dull skin of yours." She set the torch down in a bracket and pulled out a box of white clay. She started playing with it in her hands. "Eating clay will help lighten up your skin."

"I do have this annoying tan that won't go away," Sabina said.

"Okay, calm down," Brenna trilled.

"Sorry, was I being passive-aggressive?"

"One minute." Brenna yanked the sheepskin off of Sabina and stuffed the clump of clay in her hand. "Here. Eat this clay. It'll help lighten up your skin."

"Okay." Sabina tossed the clay into her mouth. It was pretty chewy. She felt like she had the end of a cow's tail in her mouth. "It has a lovely, uh, flavor?"

"No, it doesn't," Brenna said.

Sabina winced as she swallowed. "That's going to keep me up at night."

"No!" Brenna shouted. "You weren't supposed to swallow it, girl. You were supposed to chew it, then spit it onto your skin, and then fillet yourself. I mean, exfoliate yourself. You're not a fish."

"Do you think my skin can look as gorgeous as yours?" Sabina asked.

Brenna smiled and held out her arm. "Thanks. I eat clay for breakfast, brunch, and dinner."

"Brunch is a thing?" Sabina asked. She then noticed something else about Brenna's arm apart from her super pale skin. "Wow. Your veins are super bulbous."

Brenna widened her smile. "Oh, thanks. The more vivid the veins are, the better. See my arm?" She ran her fingers across what looked like navy blue branches. "My arm basically looks like my family tree because they're, like, so visible."

Sabina nearly gagged. "Ew!"

Brenna blinked. "Hello. That's, like, beautifulness."

"Not the way you just described it," Sabina gushed. "That made my stomach churn, churn like butter."

"You want the vein treatment too, right?" Brenna asked, kissing her arm.

"I mean, I guess," Sabina said, shrugging. "I want to look beautiful like you. How are you going to get my veins to pop out like yours?"

"Hold your arm out," Brenna said as she dipped her hand into a pot. "Hold still." With cupped hands, she took something out of the pot and planted her hands facedown onto Sabina's arm with a splash.

Sabina felt something wriggling beneath Brenna's hands. "What is it?"

"It's just a bloodsucking parasite worm."

When Brenna withdrew her hands, Sabina nearly jumped out of her seat at the sight of a slimy black slug locking its teeth into her skin. "Ew!" She felt the teeth, and she felt the blood running down her arm. "Are you sure this will work? What's the point here?"

"Leeches make your veins more prominent," Brenna explained, wiping her wet hands on her dress. "It's what all the fashion-forward ladies are doing these days. Are you fashion-forward or bumblebee-backward?"

Sabina eyed the pulsating leech on her arm in disgust. "Um…"

"You need more leeches," Brenna suggested, "especially in the chest area."

"That's okay," Sabina said quickly. "I'll skip that one."

"Suit yourself," Brenna said dismissively. "Is that leech sucking your blood?"

"I feel a little dizzy," Sabina said, blinking rapidly. "Does that answer your question?"

"No." Brenna scooped up a bowl and turned her back to Sabina. "Please excuse me while I go out back to my pet crocodile."

Sabina watched Brenna disappear behind a curtain. "Uh, okay." She eyed the leech and made a face. "So disgusting." With her other hand, she gently pried the leech off her arm and threw it over her shoulder. She heard the dull smack of it hitting the wall. Gross.

"I'm back!" Brenna announced.

"Oh, goodie," Sabine cooed. She was beginning to have second thoughts about this beauty boutique.

"The leech is gone!" Brenna cried.

Sabina smiled weakly. "Uh, yeah. It dissolved into my skin."

"Oh, good." Brenna held her bowl underneath Sabina's nose. "Here's some crocodile waste. Put it all over your face, and you will be restored to complete youthfulness."

Was Brenna trying to get Sabina to vomit today? The sharp, pungent smell of the bowl's contents drifted into her nose. "Hold up. Did you say crocodile waste?"

"Yes. As in excrement."

Sabina pushed the bowl out from under her nose. "I'm not putting that on my face."

Brenna huffed and set the bowl down. "Fine. Then we'll go the safer route."

"Are you saying you're giving me unsafe treatments?"

Brenna laughed. "Of course not, Sabina. All of these treatments have been tested by someone on someone with someone watching, so they're all safe. Now just relax. This next beauty treatment is very relaxing."

"Forgive me if I don't believe you," Sabina muttered.

Brenna walked around Sabina and stood behind her. "Tilt your head back a bit, girl. Keep your eyes open to their fullest extent. Pretend you're a deer in the headlights even though headlights aren't invented yet. Hold your eyes open. Are they open?"

"They're open!" Sabina shouted. "I can see you looking into my eyes in the mirror!"

"Wonderful!" Brenna cried. "Now I'll just squeeze this orange-"

"Paaaaaaain!" Sabina shouted. She shot out of the chair and tripped over the sheepskin. She clawed at her eyes and spun around like a frantic tornado. "I can't see! It stings! Brenna, what did you do?"

"Just let it seep in," Brenna said casually, scratching her forehead on the top of her scalp. "All I did was put orange juice in your eyes." She sniffed her orange and licked her lips.

"Orange juice?" Sabina yelped. "What's that supposed to do?"

"It's the go-to for ladies looking to reduce redness and make their eyes more clear and bright," Brenna recited. "Obviously," she added as she took a bite from her remaining orange.

"Do my eyes look any better now?" Sabina asked. She managed to open her eyes and looked in the mirror. "That's a no." Her eyes were completely swollen. Her pupils were dilated, and they were completely red. It looked like she had red cauliflower for eyes. "I think this beauty treatment isn't working," she concluded.

"Sabina, come on," Brenna drawled. "You can't go around looking the way you do."

"Wow, thanks."

"You at least have to have a fivehead. Let's just take care of that, and then you'll look so much better. Now, do you want me to pluck each hair out one by one? I do charge by the hour, let me inform you, so I do insist we go the other route if you don't want to spend all that money."

"What other route?" Sabina dared to ask.

"Burning."

"Oh yeah, fire," Sabina mumbled.

"So, is that a yes?" Brenna asked.

Sabina wasn't ready to say yes quite yet. "Brenna, what are your sources? Where'd you find all these supposed beauty tips? Online beauty tutorials don't exist yet."

"It's just what all the fashion-forward ladies are doing," Brenna said as if that was the obvious explanation.

"Who invented all this stuff?" Sabina cried.

"Probably the Goddess of Beauty," Brenna said.

"Like, do you have a degree in this stuff?" Sabina asked. "Or is getting degrees not a thing yet either? Seriously, I know it's the 1400s, but we gotta start inventing things, guys."

Brenna patted Sabina's shoulder. "Come back tomorrow, Sabina, when the sundial strikes four or you see four birds, and then we'll burn your hair. You'll look amazing with that super high hairline!" She kissed Sabina's cheeks in farewell and hurried her through the front curtain. "Remember," Brenna cried, waving goodbye at a miserable Sabina who was crying tears of orange juice, "tell all your friends about Brenna's Beauty Bash!"

CHAPTER 22:
THE BEARD TAX

Part 1: The Fact

Tsar Peter the Great of Russia had a lot of interests. He was a skilled military strategist, an enthusiastic sailor, and a great admirer of Western European civilizations. He brought many Western traditions to his court, including clothes, philosophy, and architecture, during his reign as emperor from 1682 to 1725 in an effort to modernize Russia.

While exploring all of these new traditions during his travels to Western Europe, Peter noticed one thing that really troubled him: men didn't have beards. His mouth fell open in complete shock at beardless men instead of the recent discoveries of a solar-centered universe and gravity. These beardless men startled the emperor so much because nearly all the men in Russia had beards, from the highest court officials to the poorest peasants. This was because the Russians believed having a beard brought you closer not to a barber, but to God.

Part 2: The Story

The discovery of these beardless societies surprised Peter, but he wasn't disgusted or offended by it. On the contrary, Peter was all for it. Despite living in a society where it was proper to grow a beard, Peter had a completely different perspective. He believed beards prevented Russia from becoming more modern. In his opinion, they represented backwardness and refusal to change. As a result, he boldly declared that Russia be beard-free.

In order to do this, Peter banned beards in 1698. The sight of clean-shaven men infuriated many people, and some even believed it to be a sign of the end times. Peter soon realized this ban was extremely unpopular. He faced a lot of backlash from nobility, peasants, and especially the church. This forced him to lift the ban, but Peter was adamant about moving on with his modernizing plans. After mulling over his situation without being able to stroke a beard while he thought, he came up with an idea to replace the beard ban. And so the beard tax was born.

How annoying would that be to cough up money if you wanted to grow a beard? Anyone who wanted to keep their beard had to pay a significant fee to the state. The tax was originally 100 rubles year, but it was later raised to 300, a crazy amount for most people. If someone couldn't pay the tax or provide a beard token when asked, they could be restrained by the police and forced to shave in public.

The beard tax received a mixed response. Some saw it as an insult to their religious beliefs, and others saw it as an opportunity to flaunt their wealth and rank by growing expensive beards. The beard tax stayed in effect even after Peter died in 1725. It wasn't fully abolished until Catherine the Great came along in 1772. Now we know why they thought Catherine was so great.

Part 3: The Breakdown

The beard ban may be an amusing historical footnote, but it gives us valuable insight into Peter the Great and his era. Peter believed that breaking with tradition was necessary to modernize Russia since he considered beards a symbol of opposition to change and backwardness.

In today's world of technology, we see similarities to this way of thinking. New technologies are seen as signs of moving forward into the future by many people today, but they're also seen by others as a danger to tradition and the way things have always been done. The beard ban serves as a timely reminder that change is frequently met with opposition and that to move forward, we must be open to fresh perspectives and be prepared to break with tradition if necessary. As we work to build a more inclusive and unprejudiced society that celebrates diversity and respects the beliefs and traditions of all people, we must be aware of the unintended effects of our actions.

CHAPTER 23:
GLADIATORS & THEIR DOLLS

Part 1: The Fact

The ancient Romans were masters of architecture, engineering, and warfare. They were also masters of making the ideal celebrity in the form of a gladiator. The ancient Romans loved gladiators. You might say they loved them to death. Gladiators were pretty much the celebrities of their time. These men, who engaged in death-defying battles at the Colosseum, were seen as fearsome warriors and as celebrities with their very own product endorsements.

Part 2: The Story

Imagine watching your favorite hero fight to the death and then leaving the battlegrounds in an excited frenzy. You look up to see a billboard of your hero, casting a giant smile while holding a bottle of olive oil in his oily hand. You're definitely buying that olive oil. You just have to ignore the fact that your favorite gladiator is now dead and gone forever, but there's always another gladiator to gush over! That was what it was like in ancient Rome. Gladiators appeared on frescoes and mosaics, advertising anything and everything from wine to bathhouses.

Brand endorsements weren't limited to only gladiators. Even the charioteers, who competed in races with horse-drawn chariots, gave their names to products and services. It was reported that Scorpus, a well-known charioteer who won over 2,000 victories, promoted a certain brand of lentils. Who wouldn't want to purchase lentils from a man who could drive a chariot like a pro?

You could even buy action figures of your favorite gladiators. These figurines were made out of clay and were super popular with kids. These toys even included miniature armor and weapons based on the actual gladiators.

Adults had their own kind of gladiator toys. Next to the toy stands selling their action figures were people selling vials of the gladiators' sweat. Wealthy women could buy the sweat and dirt scraped from the skin of a famous gladiator. The position of running behind gladiators and collecting their sweat must have had a high turnover. These scrapers even had their own scraping tool just for doing this called a strigil, which was a long, curved blade.

Women incorporated their sweaty purchases into their skincare routines. It was believed a gladiator's sweat was an aphrodisiac; the more successful a gladiator was in the arena, the more powerful their sweat was. The smellier it was too, don't forget that.

Part 3: The Breakdown

The weird beliefs and circumstance surrounding these impressive gladiators is a reminder that even the most advanced civilizations can have some really peculiar customs. It's simple to look back on ancient Rome and the gladiatorial battles in the Colosseum and think, "Wow, those people were harsh," but we should be cautious not to judge them too quickly. Who knows what future generations will think of our practices?

It's incredible that this piece of history found its way into our world now. There are, of course, tons of gladiator toys out there, from action figures and plastic armor to video games. Thankfully, though, we don't see any bottles of sweat in stores.

CHAPTER 24:
GREENWICH TIME LADY

Part 1: The Fact

The Belville's were a typical family who lived in London at the turn of the 20th century. They weren't the butcher, the baker, or even the candlestick maker, but they ran a pretty unique business selling something that you probably didn't think could be sold: the time.

Part 2: The Story

In the 19th century, time wasn't so easy to keep track of like it is now. Staring into the sun to see how late in the day it was had gotten really tiring. There weren't any digital watches or smartphones to tell the time, but people did use pocket watches. They just never worked very well. It also didn't help that Britain had no established standard time. Each town had its own local time. Talk about confusing when traveling from town to town, especially if one town said it was 11:00 in the morning and the next town ten feet away claimed it was 3:00 in the afternoon. Hopefully, the differences weren't actually that drastic.

John Henry Bellville worked at the Royal Observatory during this time. The Observatory had one thing that many people didn't have: the correct time, specifically Greenwich Mean Time. It was the country's official timekeeper. After numerous interruptions from random people traveling to the Observatory every day to get the correct time, Belville's boss told him to create some kind of service that would bring the right time to the people instead of vice versa.

Task accepted. The new service involved Belville carrying a specially corrected pocket chronometer that always had the correct time to London. The time-selling service was born, and everyone loved it.

You may be wondering why someone would spend money to adjust their watch. After all, all they had to do was ask someone else or check the clock tower to find out the time. But for some people, wearing a reliable watch was important, especially for those with jobs where keeping track of the time was important, like bankers, train drivers, and sailors. Travelers who could change their watches to GMT before leaving for a trip overseas to avoid the confusion of different time zones were particularly fond of Belville's service.

Belville continued the service for the next 20 years until he passed away. With his passing, the service could have ticked to a stop if it wanted to. The people at the Observatory had by then developed a time-distribution device that used electric clocks to send time pulses via telegraph wires to railway stations and post offices. This futuristic clock wasn't for everyone, though. Many of

Belville's customers loved the personal touch and persuaded Belville's wife, Maria, to continue the service. Almost 30 years later, their daughter, Ruth, took over from her mother. Ruth became known as the "Greenwich Time Lady."

By the beginning of the 20th century, Ruth started to face a lot of challenges with her service. There was not only the Observatory sending out time-correcting electrical pulses, but British Summer Time would soon come into effect, radios would broadcast the time, and then everyone started using those pesky things called telephones to get the time from its ingenious "speaking clock." Nevertheless, Ruth continued the service well into the 1940s and continued to have several customers.

Part 3: The Breakdown

Look how far timekeeping has come. We now take it for granted that we can always and everywhere check the time. It's hard to believe accurate timekeeping was once a luxury that only a select few could afford.

This story acts as a reminder of the power of even the smallest advances. Although the Belville family didn't create the idea of uniform time, they managed to make it widely usable. Their help made people more reliable and productive, which had an impact on society as a whole.

Even if the issues we encounter in the modern world are different, we can still learn things from the Belville family. One is that we can see the value of creativity and invention in seemingly unimportant fields like timekeeping. Also, we can appreciate the value of accuracy and dependability in our technology and services and work to justify those standards in everything we do.

CHAPTER 25:
FOR THE LOVE OF APPLES

Part 1: The Fact

Imagine you're in a convenience store. The aisle in front of you consists of a love note, a bouquet of roses, a box of chocolates, and a bright red apple. You can only buy one of these items for your valentine. You really want to show how much you love them, so which do you pick? If you wore a tunic and had a home address in ancient Greece, you'd choose the apple in a heartbeat. Why? Because in ancient Greece, throwing an apple at someone was the same as saying, "I love you."

Part 2: The Story

The roots of this literally lovestruck custom can be found in Greek mythology. According to the story, the Goddess of Conflict, Eris, was enraged when she wasn't invited to Peleus and Thetis' wedding. Wrong move, Peleus and Thetis. So, in true passive-aggressive style, Eris decided to show up late to the party and cause a commotion. Watch out, Peleus and Thetis. Eris arrived at the party with a golden apple for a wedding gift, which she hurled at three goddesses in attendance: Aphrodite, Hera, and Athena. "To the fairest" was written on the apple.

The three goddesses began arguing over who should receive the apple since they all thought they were the fairest. They decided to ask Paris, a mortal man, for his opinion on which of them was the fairest. Paris carefully considered his options, made the joke that Snow White was the fairest, and then decided Aphrodite was the fairest because she promised she'd hook him up with the most beautiful woman in the world. Unfortunately, that woman was Helen who was already married to some king of Sparta. This ultimately set off a bunch of random events that eventually led to the Trojan War, but apart from that, Peleus and Thetis ended up having a beautiful wedding.

Thanks to the story of Eris, the apple evolved into a symbol of desire and love. Catching one was taken to mean that the recipient understood how the person who threw the apple felt about them. Apples were associated with fertility and abundance, two key elements of romance and love. Also, apples were just plain easy to throw.

Part 3: The Breakdown

This early custom of throwing apples at our crushes makes us realize how crucial communication is to expressing our emotions. It's important to keep in mind that not everyone expresses or receives love in the same way. With the people we care about, it's good to be open and honest in our communication and to do so in a way they can understand and respect.

While the custom of throwing apples as a sign of love may seem comical to us today, it was a significant and profound custom in ancient Greece. Whether or not we incorporate this practice into our own life, we can appreciate the perspective it offers into the ideals and principles of the past. Maybe try it out for yourself next Valentine's Day. Just please don't throw the apple too hard, and quickly explain why you threw it. Good luck!

Part 4: The Sketch

Scooping up the folds of his heavy tunic to keep himself from tripping, Sebastian rushed down the hallway past the spiraling columns into the crowded classroom. He quickly slowed down to a casual stride as he passed Chloe and Zoe, who were excitedly chattering away with their heads drawn together so no one could hear them. Sebastian tried to keep his eyes locked forward, but he couldn't help but peek at Chloe as he passed her. To his surprise, she looked right up at him and gave him a bright smile. Sebastian's eyes widened, and he picked up the pace to his seat. He looked back at Chloe. She had resumed her excited conversation with Zoe.

Sebastian slid forward in his seat and proceeded to pound his head against his marble desk. That was so embarrassing.

"Sebastian?"

Sebastian yelped and jumped up in his seat. He spun around and saw his friend, Orion, looking at him strangely. "Why'd you scare me like that, Orion?"

"I didn't do it on purpose," Orion replied. "Why'd you run past Chloe like that? I thought you liked her?"

"I thought I did, too," Sebastian said glumly. "Actually, I still think I do."

A flurry of bright green linen entered the room, and their teacher, Miss Athena, came to a halt in front of the classroom. "Hello, everyone!" she said cheerfully, beaming at her unenthusiastic class. "Welcome to philosophy! Don't worry. There's no fee to join philosophy!" She chuckled at her joke but quickly stopped when no one else laughed with her. "It's going to be one of those days," she sighed. "Well, anyway…" Miss Athena reached down and lifted something onto her desk. It was a statue of a head with a long beard and pupil-less eyes. "Can anyone guess who this is?"

"Is it me?" a student named Alexander asked.

Miss Athena frowned. "Obviously not. It's Plato. Surprise! He's our guest speaker today!"

"How can a statue speak to us?" Orion asked.

Miss Athena frowned again. "What? No. The statue isn't the speaker. The real Plato will be speaking. Are you excited?"

No one made a sound.

Miss Athena threw her hands up in defeat. "Fine. Never mind. Free period." She grabbed the head and scuttled out of the classroom.

As soon as she left, Sebastian reached into his satchel. "Hey, Orion. Look what I have." He took out a shining green apple and placed it between him and Orion on the desk. "Do you know what it is?"

"Obviously," Orion said, poking the apple. "Why'd you bring it to school?" He leaned forward and whispered teasingly, "Does somebody have a crush?"

Sebastian pointed to himself. "Yeah, *I* do. Come on, Orion. That's why I have the apple."

Orion rolled his eyes. "I know. I was just teasing you, but apparently you're being all too serious right now. Who do you have a crush on as if I didn't know?"

Sebastian looked over his shoulder toward Chloe and Zoe. All he could see was the back of Chloe's flowing black hair, but he couldn't help but feel soft and mushy inside. She made him feel that way every time he saw her. He knew it had to be love.

"Can I help you?"

Sebastian almost stopped breathing. Chloe had turned around without him noticing. How long had he been staring at her? He nervously cleared his throat. "Uh, uh, do you have the time?"

Chloe snorted. "I'm not the Greenwich Time Lady."

"Like, oh my Sparta," Zoe cackled behind Chloe. "Like, Chloe, I think someone likes you!" She burst out giggling. "I can't blame him since we're so popular!"

"We're so popular!" Chloe cooed, turning back to Zoe. "We're basically like Hera and Demeter right now."

Zoe suddenly stopped giggling. "Ew. Which one of us is Demeter? Better not be me. I don't want to be some goddess who sits around watching over crops and grains. I'd rather be Hera."

"Seriously?" Chloe gasped. "You'd rather be someone who goes around turning people into heifers?"

Zoe bit her lip in thought. "I'm beginning to see how unrealistic these goddesses are." She peered over Chloe's shoulder and narrowed her eyes. "What, boy?"

Sebastian jumped, nearly knocking his apple off his desk. "Nothing!" He turned back to Orion, who had grabbed the apple to keep it from zooming across the room. "Orion, I'm nervous."

"About what?" Orion asked. Before he could say anything else, a girl in a lumpy tunic pinned together by what looked like over a dozen golden brooches in the shape of a heart appeared between him and Sebastian. "Sophelia!"

"Hey, guys," Sophelia simmered. She looked back and forth between the two boys with a smile as big as the sun. "Is anyone excited about the school dance? I mean, I'm so ready since all we learn in school is how to sing and dance and make instruments and occasionally bludgeon, so I just know this dance will be so fun!" She casually leaned over to Orion, who had to try not to fall out of his seat to avoid her touch. "Are you going to ask me to the dance, O'Brien?" she asked.

"My name isn't O'Brien," Orion said, squirming in his seat. "This isn't ancient Ireland."

"My bad." Sophelia suddenly gasped. Her eyes traveled down to the apple in Orion's hands. Her face lit up, and she started hopping in place out of irrepressible joy. "Are you going to throw that apple at me?" she squealed. "Do you like me?"

Orion looked at the apple and quickly pushed it over to Sebastian. "No. Sorry."

Sophelia deflated like a balloon. She shot Orion a scathing look and then looked over at Alexander sitting at the desk behind them, scribbling something on a clay tablet. "Hey, Alexander. Are you going to ask me to the dance? Do you have an apple to announce your love for me?"

Alexander looked up with a distant expression on his face. "What? Oh, sorry. I was busy sketching out the landmasses in the Ambracian Gulf, which is difficult since there's no land since it's water."

Sophelia snatched the stylus out of his hand. "I know you're dumb, but I want someone to ask me to the dance. Go find an apple and throw it at me so you can pronounce your love for me and take me to the dance. Do it now!"

Alexander gulped underneath Sophelia's glowering gaze and shakily stood up. He patted down his tunic and walked around his desk. "I'm going to borrow that, thanks." He grabbed Sebastian's apple.

"Sock it to me!" Sophelia yelled, shutting her eyes and holding out her arms.

Alexander lifted the apple but before throwing it, he spun around to face another girl. "I actually wanted to ask Chloe to the dance."

"No!" Sebastian shouted in a garbled tone. He threw the excess folds of his white tunic over his head and wailed like a forlorn ghost. "This can't be happening!"

"Calm down, dude," Orion said.

Alexander approached Chloe and tapped her on the shoulder. "Hey, Chloe?"

Chloe spun around and looked up at Alexander. "Oh my Sparta. It's Alexander."

"Like, oh my Sparta!" Zoe giggled uncontrollably. "He's definitely not Alexander the Great because he doesn't dress great!" She started giggling so hard that saliva went flying everywhere. She suddenly stopped cackling to say, "Wait. I'm wearing one of these ugly tunics too."

Alexander held the apple up in front of Chloe's face. "Uh, I have this apple."

Chloe eyed the apple and nodded. "I can see. What are you going to do with it?"

"Throw it at her!" Zoe screeched with maniacal eyes.

"No!" Sebastian screeched even louder from beneath his tunic.

In one abrupt movement, Alexander hoisted his arm upward. To his surprise, the apple flew out of his hand before he could throw it. He yelped after realizing he had just smacked Chloe right in the face instead. "I'm so sorry!"

Chloe screamed and held her jaw. "You just, like, punched me!"

Alexander stumbled backward. "I'm sorry! I raised my arm, and it ricocheted off your face!"

"That's a rico-shame," Zoe said, shaking her head. "I really wanted to see some love action going on."

"The apple!" Sebastian suddenly yelled. "It's mine!" He flew out from under his tunic and dropped to the ground. Lying on his stomach, he scanned the floor for the missing apple. "Where'd it go?" Then he saw it. The small green fruit lay beside the desk in the back. He barreled forward and grabbed the apple. He jumped up and raised the apple into the air. "Triumph!" He noticed everyone staring at him. "Excuse that outburst."

Zoe snorted. "Wow, Chloe. Can you believe that guy? I mean, look at his tunic. It looks like he's wearing a blanket."

Sebastian pressed the apple against his chest and shuffled back to his desk. He plopped into his seat and moaned. "Orion, what am I going to do?"

"Weren't you going to throw your apple at someone? That was a weird thing to say."

"I want to throw it at Chloe," Sebastian whispered. "But you saw Alexander. He tried, and she denounced him."

"He also punched her," Orion reminded him. "Just throw the apple at her. I'm sure she likes you too, and I'm sure she'd want to go to the dance with you."

"I'm frightened," Sebastian quivered.

Orion rapped his knuckles on the desk impatiently. "Why are you scared? You're just throwing an apple at someone. It's no big deal. I could throw an apple at anyone I liked if I wanted to."

Sophelia appeared at his side again. "Then do it, Orion." She stepped back and held her arms out. "Throw an apple in my face, like, really hard. Do it! Give me a black eye! Do it!"

"That's it." Orion stood up and grabbed the apple out of Sebastian's hand. "Sophelia, I'm going to throw this apple, but not at you. I'm going to throw it at Zoe."

"… think anyone will throw an apple at me, Chloe?" Zoe was saying while playing with the clasps that fastened her

139

cape around her neck. "It's such an enduring act of love and something totally accepted in society. I so want someone to throw an apple at me, but I also don't because it'd totally hurt. Also, I'm intolerant to fruit specimens-"

"Hey, Zoe?"

Zoe looked up with her mouth hanging open and stared at Orion.

Chloe saw the apple in Orion's hand and squealed. "Like, Zoe!"

"Like, what, Chloe?"

Orion lifted his arm and threw the apple.

Zoe screamed like she had just been uncontrollably tickled and shut her eyes to brace herself. After a few seconds, she opened one eye and looked around. "Uh, did Orion just throw an apple at me?"

Chloe shrugged and looked around. "Something flew past us. Not sure if it was Pegasus or not."

"Oops." Orion smiled apologetically and scampered behind the desk to get the apple that had sailed right over Zoe's head instead of hitting her. "Sorry. Let's try again." Orion jogged back to position with his apple. "This is why I take singing and musical instrument-making lessons instead of enrolling with the warriors. I have no hand-eye coordination. Oomph!" He threw the apple again.

Zoe screamed. "Oh my Sparta!" This time, the apple hit her in the shoulder.

"I did it!" Orion shouted ecstatically.

"Zoe!" Chloe cried giddily. "Orion threw an apple at you!"

Zoe looked stunned. "Oh my Sparta." She grabbed Orion's hand and held it against her heart. "Oh, my love. You thee there did throw an apple at me?"

"I did," Orion gushed, his heart beating fast.

Zoe leaned in closer to Orion. "This means we shall be together forever."

"Do you want to come to the dance with me?" Orion asked, his lips inches away from Zoe's.

"Yes," Zoe breathed, her breath intermingling with Orion's like two clouds of fog uniting into one single swarm of dew. "Wait a minute." She let go of Orion's hand. "What's the theme of the dance this year? The acropolis?"

"I think the theme is ancient," Chloe said.

"We're already in ancient Greece," Zoe snapped. "How can the theme be even more ancient than ancient Greece?"

"Then it's probably, like, cornfield or bathhouse," Chloe guessed. "Or volcano."

"What do volcanoes have to do with us?"

"Nothing yet," Chloe replied mysteriously.

"Chloe!"

Everyone in the classroom looked up to see Sebastian standing on a desk. Like a statue of a god, he stood with his arm in the air, holding the love-stricken apple. "Orion has given me strength to carry out my plan with my apple. *My* apple. Guys, stop taking it from me."

Chloe stood up and looked at Sebastian with wide eyes. "Sebastian, do you mean? Do you truly mean?"

"Yes." Sebastian wound his arm back. "Brace yourself!"

"Throw it!" Chloe shrieked.

Sebastian hurled the apple as hard as he could. He shouted in triumph as it struck Chloe right in the face. "Yes!" He jumped off the desk and ran over to Chloe who, for some reason, was lying sprawled out on the floor. He looked down at her and frowned since she didn't get up and fall into his waiting arms. "Chloe?"

Zoe tapped Chloe's head with her foot. "I think she's unconscious."

"Why'd you throw the apple so hard?" Orion hollered.

"I don't know," Sebastian said, shrugging.

"Oh, my head…"

"Chloe!"

Sebastian helped Chloe sit up. He winced when he saw chunks of apple lodged in her face, mixed with blood streaming down her nose. "Uh, do you feel okay?"

Chloe licked her lips. "I feel traumatized but just fine apart from that." She peeled a piece of apple skin off her face. When she saw it, her eyes widened, realizing what had just happened. "Zoe! I got hit by an apple too!"

Zoe grabbed her and hugged her. "Oh my Sparta, Chloe! We're, like, twinning right now!"

Sebastian pushed Zoe aside and grabbed Chloe in a hug. "Chloe, I announce my unending love for you. This means we'll be together forever!"

Chloe wiped blood out of her eyes. "Or at least til the dance is over because I feel like I'll be in the hospital for a while afterward."

Stunned by what Chloe had just said, Sebastian let go of her and jumped up. "What? We won't be together forever? I thought I pronounced my love for you?"

"Listen, bud," Chloe said, holding her head, "I'm not sure if I'm ready for that kind of commitment right now."

"Oh." Sebastian nodded, trying to understand. The excitement of the apple proposal was beginning to melt away. "Okay. Well, when you're ready, just throw an apple at me."

"Okay, I'll let you know."

"Oh, I'll know when I get struck by an apple."

Chloe spit out some apple. She didn't look as exhilarated about getting bombarded in the face with a fruity rock anymore. "You bet you'll know. I'll throw an apple at you so hard you'll end up way up there in Zeus' house!"

BONUS CHAPTER:
THE TRACTOR SHIFT

Part 1: The Fact

Welcome to the bonus chapter! Weird things don't just happen in history, you know. This event happened as recently as March 2021 and involved the shrinking of an entire country. A farmer in Belgium was going about his usual farm activities when he stumbled upon a large stone with some faded inscriptions. Frustrated that it was in his way, he dug it up with his tractor and moved it. Little did he know he moved a 200-year-old stone border marker, consequently changing the size of two countries.

Part 2: The Story

The border between France and Belgium dates back to the Treaty of Kortrijk in 1820. It hadn't moved for two centuries. The farmer, who remains nameless, was tending to his crops when it all began. He saw an old stone marker in his way with the year 1819 etched into it. Making the decision to take matters into his own hands, he used his tractor to move it out of the way rather than work around it.

The farmer unknowingly moved the marker almost eight feet deeper into French territory. A couple of months later, a group of Frenchman wandering the countryside and conveniently checking the border markers encountered the displaced marker. They immediately felt something was wrong. They checked their handy maps and discovered it wasn't where it should have been. If they hadn't come along, the stone probably would never have been noticed since it was in such an isolated spot in a forest. Unfortunately, they didn't have a tractor on hand to move the stone back. They couldn't move it themselves since it weighed between 300 and 600 pounds.

When they heard the news, French officials were understandably astonished to find the discrepancy and contacted their Belgian counterparts. To find out what had happened, they started a joint investigation. It was soon apparent that the border had been changed. The mistake was taken in good humor by both countries. Belgium officials reached out to the farmer to move the stone back. As far as we know, there hasn't yet been any confirmation that the farmer moved the stone back.

Part 3: The Breakdown

This incident will definitely be considered as one of the "weird thing in history" 200 years from now. Although it may appear like a scene from a comedy show, the mistaken shifting of the French-Belgian border speaks to some important issues. For centuries, tensions between nations have been fueled by border and territorial conflicts. Land and resource disputes have caused many wars and conflicts throughout history, from ancient empires to contemporary nation-states. It serves as a reminder that even seemingly unimportant things like marker stones can have tremendous effects.

AFTERWORD

How weird was that? This definitely wasn't your typical history book. Putting a quirky spin on things is always a fun idea. We're not only learning about history and how it helped shape our world today, but we're also left with a smile. It's the perfect combination.

The weird things that happened long ago remind us there's no such thing as a single human experience. Instead, there have been a lot of unique and odd episodes throughout history, each with its own batch of causes and results. By looking at these events, we can learn more about the long range of human experiences that have existed and still do.

Learning about these crazy events can challenge our views and thoughts about what's normal and acceptable in society. Something might have been unheard of in the past but common now like a smartphone. It proves how society is always changing, and it's not going to stop.

Reading stories like these is a reminder that history is more complex than a straightforward march toward advancement and enlightenment. Instead, it's a crazy ride with many unforeseen turns. We can better comprehend the intricacy of the past and the present by accepting the oddity of history.

Finally, it's just plain fun researching weird things. It gives us a chance to explore the unexpected and the often forgotten aspects of our world. There are a ton of odd practices and events. Hopefully, you learned about some weird things you didn't know about.

We hope you enjoyed *Weird Things in History and Why the Heck They Happened.* Together, we traveled through some of the more extraordinary and obscure historical events that hopefully raised some eyebrows (unless you took the "Love That Fivehead" chapter seriously and shaved them off). From luxurious prickly fruits and beavers on the moon to miracle ketchup and dumb glass people, we saw that fact can definitely be stranger than fiction.

We all know there is a lot of weird history out there. Believe it or not, stories like the ones presented here might not even be on a bookshelf or an online article. If you have a past family member who was involved in some kind of super weird historical event or know of something crazy that happened in your community long ago, we'd love to hear about it! When you leave your review of this book, share your weird family history by using *#myweirdhistory* in the review. Your story could end up in a future installment of *Weird Things in History and Why the Heck They Happened!* Thanks for getting weird with us!

IMAGE SOURCES

"Lunar animals and other objects Discovered by Sir John Herschel in his observatory at the Cape of Good Hope and copied from sketches in the Edinburgh Journal of Science." *Picryl,* 1835, https://picryl.com/media/lunar-animals-and-other-objects-discovered-by-sir-john-herschel-in-his-observatory-1. Accessed May 20, 2023.

"Runners forming at the start line of the 1904 Olympics Marathon Race." *GetArchive,* https://garystockbridge617.getarchive.net/amp/media/runners-forming-at-the-start-line-of-the-1904-olympics-marathon-race-3fd012, Accessed May 20, 2023.

"Konishi Hirosada - Naozane's Challenge - Walters 95714." *GetArchive,* https://jenikirbyhistory.getarchive.net/amp/media/konishi-hirosada-naozanes-challenge-walters-95714-1196d7, Accessed May 20, 2023.

Coyne, Jason. "Kilroy Was Here - Washington DC WWII Memorial - Jason Coyne.jpg." Wikimedia Commons, 2006, https://commons.wikimedia.org/wiki/File:Kilroy_Was_Here_-_Washington_DC_WWII_Memorial_-_Jason_Coyne.jpg, Accessed May 20, 2023.

"Pineapple Hendrik Danckerts." *Rolling Harbour Abaco,* https://rollingharbour.com/2012/07/24/pineapples-symbols-of-welcome-wealth-also-delicious/. Accessed May 20, 2023.

"Henry Bernard Chalon - A favorite pug (1802)." *GetArchive,* 1802, https://jenikirbyhistory.getarchive.net/amp/media/henry-bernard-chalon-a-favorite-pug-1802-b16b00, Accessed May 20, 2023.

"In 1939, Swallowing Live Goldfish Became a Wildly Popular Fad Among College Students." *Vintage Everyday,* https://www.vintag.es/2022/07/goldfish-swallowing-craze.html. Accessed May 20, 2023.

"'Vampires' in Ancient Literature." *Caesar the Day,* 2012, https://caesartheday.wordpress.com/2012/07/08/vampires-in-ancient-literature/, Accessed May 20, 2023.

"Remembering Lawn Chair Larry." *Overdrive*, https://
www.overdriveonline.com/overdrive-extra/article/14882831/
remembering-lawn-chair-larry. Accessed May 20, 2023.

"Princess Alexandra Amalie of Bavaria." *Wikimedia Commons*, 1847,
https://commons.wikimedia.org/wiki/
File:Princess_Alexandra_Amalie_of_Bavaria.jpg. Accessed May 20, 2023.

"Caligula and Incitatus." *All Posters*, https://en.wikipedia.org/wiki/
Incitatus#/media/File:Cal%C3%ADgula_e_Incitato.jpg. Accessed May
20, 2023.

"Jim LeBlanc inside the vacuum chamber." *Cult of Weird*, https://
www.cultofweird.com/science/1966-moon-suit-experiment/. Accessed
May 20, 2023.

"Paris during the war." *Culture Trip*, https://theculturetrip.com/europe/
france/paris/articles/a-second-paris-was-built-during-wwi-to-confuse-
german-bombers/. Accessed May 20, 2023.

"Edison's Talking Dolls Can Now Provide The Soundtrack To Your
Nightmares." *NPR*, 2015, https://www.npr.org/sections/thetwo-way/
2015/05/05/404445211/edisons-talking-dolls-can-now-provide-the-
soundtrack-to-your-nightmares. Accessed May 20, 2023.

"Example of a ketchup advertisement in the 1800's." *Medium*, 2021,
https://perfectmess.medium.com/ketchup-was-sold-as-medicine-in-
the-1800s-8b601329bc28. Accessed May 20, 2023.

"The novel Gadsby, published in 1939, is the longest book ever published
that does not include the letter 'e'." *Shortpedia*, https://
www.shortpedia.com/en-in/did-you-know/did-you-know-facts/the-
novel-gadsby-published-in-1939-is-the-longest-book-ever-published-that-
does-not-include-the-letter-e-1631619645. Accessed May 20, 2023.

"James Wide and his pet assistant Jack the baboon." *STSTQ Media*,
https://www.ststworld.com/jack-the-baboon/. Accessed May 20, 2023.

"Bonaparte by Wicar 1808." *Wikimedia Commons*, https://
commons.wikimedia.org/wiki/File:Bonaparte_by_Wicar_1808.JPG.
Accessed May 20, 2023.

"WelbeckAbbeyJonesViews1829." *Wikimedia Commons*, https://commons.wikimedia.org/wiki/File:WelbeckAbbeyJonesViews1829.jpg. Accessed May 20, 2023.

"Portrait of a woman." *Fashion History Timeline*, 1445, https://fashionhistory.fitnyc.edu/beauty-adorns-virtue-italian-renaissance-fashion/. Accessed May 20, 2023.

"Charles W. Bray '25 and E. Glenn Weaver. Undergraduate Alumni Records (AC199)." *University Archives*, https://universityarchives.princeton.edu/2017/04/the-cat-telephone/. Accessed May 20, 2023.

"Peter the Great." *Royal Museums Greenwich*, https://www.rmg.co.uk/stories/topics/peter-great. Accessed May 20, 2023.

"Detail of Gladiator mosaic, a Thraex (left) fighting a Murmillo (right), Römerhalle, Bad Kreuznach, Germany (8196070427)." *Wikimedia Commons*, 2012, https://commons.wikimedia.org/wiki/File:Detail_of_Gladiator_mosaic,_a_Thraex_%28left%29_fighting_a_Murmillo_%28right%29,_Römerhalle,_Bad_Kreuznach,_Germany_%288196070427%29.jpg. Accessed May 20, 2023.

"Ruth Belville." *Alchetron*, 2022, https://alchetron.com/Ruth-Belville. Accessed May 29, 2923.

"WHY MEN OF ANCIENT GREECE PROPOSED TO THEIR BELOVED BY THROWING AN APPLE AT HER." *Greece High Definition*, 2012, https://www.greecehighdefinition.com/blog/2021/2/20/why-men-of-ancient-greece-proposed-to-their-beloved-by-throwing-an-apple-at-her. Accessed May 20, 2023.

Lavaux, David. "The border was marked out by stone markers which have remained in place." *BBC*, 2021, https://www.bbc.com/news/world-europe-56978344. Accessed May 20, 2023.

ABOUT THE AUTHOR

Pablo has a passion for history and a knack for humor. Born with an insatiable curiosity, he has spent countless hours diving into the depths of the past, uncovering fascinating stories and forgotten anecdotes. Pablo's unique talent lies in his ability to blend historical facts with a witty sense of humor, creating entertaining narratives that transport readers to different eras while leaving them with a smile on their faces. Whether delving into the adventures of ancient civilizations or shedding light on little-known historical events, Pablo's work promises a delightful blend of knowledge and laughter, making history come alive in a way that is both engaging and entertaining.

Made in the USA
Las Vegas, NV
01 December 2023

81932833R00095